"Paul Bennett taught me many ways that words can make a difference. He impressed upon me the importance of precision and economy in word selection.

The poems of *Appalachian Mettle* are faithful to his teaching, and much more. His poetry is at the core of his character and his life-style.

The wisdom and experience of his compassionate observations are in unity with the integrity of his poetic expression."

—Richard G. Lugar
United States Senator

"Paul Bennett's poetry is deceptively simple. He finds meaning in everyday details and events that make up a person's life and mettle. As his student, I learned to look at the ordinary and consider it extraordinary. This is his legacy."

— Susan Peterson, President
Susan Peterson Productions, Inc.

"I grew up feeling I never had the right apple to give my teacher. I sat in class wondering how I could impress my instructor, how I could avoid the sharp question, how I could be prepared for the unannounced quiz. If I sat in the back, hidden by knowledgeable students, I could ease my way through an education. That was until I met Paul Bennett about 35 years ago at Denison University in his English class on poetry. His enthusiasm, his wit and knowledge, and his intellectual persistence forced me to attention where I have stood ever since. Was I part of a team that gave something back to Paul when our company produced the film "Dead Poets Society"? I hope so. And what irony that I, one of his average students, has been asked to write a few words in a book of his poetry!

As Poet-In-Residence at this small Midwestern university, Paul jolted me to literary consciousness by his imagery, his power in use of words to convey deep feelings and his sweeping observations and strong convictions.

It was Paul who taught me, and several generations, that poetry was not solely the province of the fabled dead, but that poetry lives in the contemporary world of wonder and imagination.

I envy all who will enjoy Paul Bennett's work here for the first time, and I challenge first time Bennett readers not to be totally captive by the end of the first few pages. I invite all readers to join Paul's "Live poets society".

— **Michael D. Eisner**
Chairman and C.E.O.
The Walt Disney Company

"As a writer and poet, Paul Bennett exposes the extraordinary in the ordinary. He enables us to look at life more clearly through his keen, gentle eyes. My own life has been shaped, in many ways, by his perspective on the world."

— **Sara Fritz**
Managing Editor
Congressional Quarterly

"*Appalachian Mettle* is not only the definition of a place, it is the definition of a life. It is a life spent richly in quiet observation—a life we long for, the way we long for all things we fear can no longer be. These poems are true as the land they were born from, deep as the soul who wrote them down."

— **Pam Houston, author**
Cowboys Are My Weakness
Washington Square Press
Pocket Books

"To love one bit of soil is to know the earth," observes Paul Bennett in a poem. This collection celebrates his lifelong, devoted tending of the literal and imaginative ground Paul Bennett holds dear, and the gleaned knowledge of our human selves is his readers' gain.

— **Kathy Mangan, author**
Above the Tree Line
Carnegie Mellon University Press

Appalachian Mettle

by
Paul Bennett

Paul Bennett

Published by:

savage **PRESS**

Box 115, Superior, WI 54880 (715) 394-9513

Second Edition
Printed in 1998

© Copyright 1997
Paul Bennett

Cover Photo © 1997
Harriet D. Lattimer

ISBN 1-886028-27-3

Library of Congress Catalog Card Number: 97-068167

Printed in the U.S.A.
at
Morris Publishing
Kearney, NE

Table of Contents

Part I

Part II

Table of Contents

Table of Contents

Narrative Poems

Acknowledgments

Of the poems in APPALACHIAN METTLE, these have had prior publication: "Memorial to W.H. Auden" in *Centennial Review*; "Of Voices: The Give and Take" and "Fishing Again the Evolutionary Stream" in *Gambit Magazine*; "My Old Man" in *The Georgia Review*; "Clyde," "Stuck on Open," "A Neighborly Visit," "Grapes," and "Husband and Wife" in *The Christian Science Monitor*; "Essay: On Schools" in *Aspen Leaves*; "On Reforming Education," "A Heave-Ho Horseman," and "A Valentine for Jeanne" in *Delmar*; "Coyote" and "In the Shadow of the Pine" in *America*; "Third Man in the Ring," "Canoeing," and "Light Thoughts" in *The Journal*; "The Ravenous Bed" in *The Blackbird Circle*; "One Word" in *Analect*; "On Carolinian Sand" in *The Sandlapper*; and "The Conference on War and Peace" in *The Gamut*.

Of the narrative poems, "The Saga of Sam Whitfield" appeared in *The Beloit Poetry Journal*; "Building a House" as a chapbook by *Limekiln Press*; "Kirk's Hospital Visit" (under title "Hospital") in *Loon;* "On Newfoundland Rocks" in *Agni: Boston University Review*; and "On John Yahres' Civil War Diary" in the anthology *The Soil Is Suited To The Seed*.

Dedication

FOR APPALACHIANS EVERYWHERE

and especially for

Charlie and Ida

Bill and Lisa

and theirs:

Christina, Lindsay, Michael, Steven and Kittery

Foreword

It begins with the naming, the words, the poet's tools, nearly every poem contains a word we did not know, had never used. And the words flower into crevices, forcing open what time has sealed. Paul Bennett was born in a time, before the century's wars and in a place—rural eastern Ohio—that is so deeply American we can barely comprehend it at his century's close: the language of small towns and large families, of farms and factories, the depression and the war, the language of caring for field and flower, wife and continuity. It's even a place where the myths still can touch us, where the long-retired Cy Young farms and names a sickly calf Ty Cobb to help him survive.

This is a book of tough testimony, lest one think it celebrates only the springtime and vanishings, only the satisfactions of a life well lived. Bennett's is a wintery testament, a magician's conjured world of memory, of engagement with dark and light that few can match but many will recognize.

Many, many people, from all realms of life, know Paul Bennett; he has shaped everything and everyone he's touched. But few, I suspect, know the Paul Bennett of *Appalachian Mettle*. The sly farmer has hidden his finest vintage. This book is a luscious surprise, a great harvest, a feast served by a master.

— Clark Blaise, Director
International Writing Program
The University of Iowa
Iowa City, Iowa

Part I

Appalachian Mettle

Paul Bennett

Memorial to W.H. Auden (1907 - 1973)

The words of a dead man
are modified in the guts of the living.
— W.H. Auden

The convoluted face unfolds,
a poet's voice is still today;
time's great wrinkle wraps his tongue
but I hear him repeating
his anecdote of the Young Man:
"The Young Man came to me saying,
'I have a message for the world—
would you advise me to be a poet?'
I could not say to him,
'No, you should not be a poet,'
but I would have felt better
had he said to me, 'I love words,
and loving words, would you advise me
to be a poet?' Then I would have said,
'Hell yes, poetry needs you,
the world needs you and your words.'
You see, I have always assumed
each man farms his own integrity."

Appalachian Mettle

Mary Eva

Growing up on an Ohio farm,
a sapling girl, eldest of four children,
Welsh and German crossed with vixen,
she dropped out from the country school
where she had skipped one grade already,
when she had thrust upon her her father's work:
delivering rural mail twelve miles each day.

Climbing stony, hoof-sparking hills,
traversing long, sandy, leafy lanes,
one with her mare in heat she rode
one full year and one bright summer,
chased Indian summer into winter,
and steadily plowed deep drifted snows,
numb-fingered fists locked on frozen reins.

The March day leather-leaved bloodroot bloomed
she picked a man almost randomly,
as from grain bin she had grabbed up
ears of corn, ignoring husk and cob
to feed the fiery animal she rode.
"Son, your father, as you know,
never quite got his tail on track."

For him—student at three colleges,
master of English, Latin, church history,
Irish-Anglo dreamer awaiting God's call
(*Emerson* was his middle name),
man of principles too large for his time—
she sacrificed youth, beauty, body:
conceiving, birthing, rearing eight children.

Paul Bennett

Her house in order, she hired out as a maid:
washing, ironing, cooking, serving,
carpentering, paperhanging, gardening, canning,
painting, tending the sick, baby sitting—
one who could cajole and wheedle, caress
but strike in anger; who,
seeing something done, could do it better.

To such a one, her seventh child, sixth son,
sickly at birth, I was but one mouth more
and could not have been, by any reckoning,
worth the bother of my tending,
but she held me close, breast fed,
lovingly looked after and comforted,
dreamed over, prayed for, believed in.

My cradle she wrought upon Shaker model:
skeleton canoe—wheels at prow and barrow handles—
walnut reproduction of her own rib cage,
warm from her heart, whose strong oomp-beat
became the measure of my life,
our shared hum of partial happiness
more constant than birds and bees.

Rehearsing eighty-four prodigious years
she talked far into July's hottest night
as we journeyed around the world she'd made,
past sunrises and sunsets, traveling farther
and farther with each uttered thought
until a star plunging from midnight sky
left behind a silence, blue and dark.

Appalachian Mettle

An Irish Father

American mongrel, profoundly Irish, my father
blamed his lack of height on his boyhood bedroom
where as he grew he bumped his head on the rafters.

With glee he said: "I got to live close to the sky,
sun, moon, stars, the sifting snow;
I never found roof beams heavy on heart or mind."

Another time he explained: "What I owned was in my
head so I kept fists and feet close to guard it well."

"Will I be small, taking after you?" I asked.
He said: "You may be what you will yourself to be."

It took me years to appreciate his Irishry,
his word games, his ability to foretell outcomes.

When his friend Sean Hennesey married a widow
who had grown sons, Father said: "Time alone
will tell how Hennie's marriage will work out,
the test will come when he begins to doubt her
motives: did she marry him for love or for her sons'
sake, their futures?"

Within the year Sean Hennesey came to Father
asking that very question. Father said quietly:
"Such a question, like many, can never be
answered, but plainly, Hennie, it doesn't become you
as a man to ask it. Put it from your mind with
dogmatic snap."

Paul Bennett

The day I shouldered our double-bitted ax and
marched off to help my school chum Pierce Grabling
chop firewood, I was cursed and sent home by Mr.
Grabling, who shouted: "Don't you dare let Pierce
touch that weapon—a double-bitted ax is more
dangerous than dynamite."

When I told Father what had happened, he said:
"A double-bitted ax in a fool's hands is
dangerous—it asks to be mastered. I'm afraid your
friend Pierce is condemned to take life's close shaves
with a safety razor."

Years later, when I was at sea in the Navy,
word came that Pierce, trapped in the Air Force,
too tense to become either pilot or navigator,
had slit his throat with a straight-edged razor.

On a Sunday near the close of his long life Father and
I walked a field in search of Indian relics, and he told
me how much he anticipated our finding amid the
stars, other civilizations, other beings, bodies,
minds—lives predicated upon novel principles.

"Think of what it will do for us," he mused,
"what blindness will fall from our eyes,
what garbage will cram our refuse trucks,
what vanities freight the breeze,
how worthless may prove our wisest ways."

He ranted on as Irishmen do, asserting he got
what little he knew from Irish history, Irish myth,
and never felt a lesser wit for borrowing it.

Appalachian Mettle

A Family Tale

I knew she had been my father's teacher
long before she became surrogate mother
to four of us six boys, as though
through sons she could touch the father.
In a white-faced moment, stopping blood spurting
where a hay fork pierced my leg,
she buried her lips in my hair and confided:
"But for fate I would have been your mother."

I would say of our flesh and blood mother,
by her busy hands she reared all eight,
garnering food, fuel, shelter, clothing,
burdened by an Irish-English dreamer
who took his stand upon books, and, politely put,
never quite set his feet on the ground.
Before and after the act of love
their low-pitched arguments rose and fell
like a two-edged sword lopping ears
through thin walls of a cardboard house.

I would honor all that was Aunt Sarah's:
cattle, horses, sheep, and barns,
white picket fence, immaculate lawn, tall maples,
the pillared porch and high-ceilinged rooms,
three hundred and nineteen acres
of streams, falls, hills, fields, woods—
the extra acre given for the township school,
one room housing eight grades, "Where," she said,
"your father was the brightest lad I ever taught.
Your father...your father..."

Paul Bennett

I celebrate two heroic, strong-willed women—
one keen as a vixen barking, defending
her den of nursing needle-toothed pups,
and the other in modulated teacher's voice saying:
"Do well in your studies, son. Read, think,
and write, and I will come to hear you speak.
Your father...your father..."
Here the facts leave off and myth begins.

Appalachian Mettle

Of Voices: The Give and Take

At noon on the long drive south
when you pull into a restaurant,
what do you say to the man
whose shoulders you rode to the world,
whose sweat defined house as home,
who read Latin for your Latin teacher,
whose wisdom seemed infinite?
You take his arm, steer him to the john,
re-enter the dining room, and wait,
and wait. And what do you say
when you return to the john
to find him standing, facing the wall?

You do his zipper and turn him to the urinal.

You both wait and wait: a dozen drops,
a dozen more. Finally he says, "That's all."
You push the slight worm that gave you life
under surplus shirt-tail, work the zipper,
turn and wash two sets of hands
and dry them beneath the blower.
You hold the doors and enter the dining room,
order lunch for two, and eat slowly.
Then you say, "Well Skipper, are we ready
to hit the long road once more?"

"Not yet," he says. "I have to go again."

You redo the doors, the zipper—
down, and up—wash and dry two sets of hands;

then you get him into coat and hat
and help him to the car.
And what do you say when he stops
beside the car to remark:
"Once I was the man and you were the boy,
now you are the man and I am the boy"—
more than content the voice, the voice
that your voice will forever echo.

Appalachian Mettle

My Old Man

Body tubed to bottles,
wrists strapped to steel,
head gone to stone,
still your eyes, blue and wild,
roamed over fields
where earth clacked under hoofs
and the rank dust rose.

"That goddamned colt—
he kicked me down!"
Your bloodless lips shaped
a pleased surprise,
and your boy's breath,
saved over eighty years,
raced from your bony chest.

The sound of hoofs echoed,
going away from the barn,
down the long locust lane
to green Laurel Creek,
and the noise was liquid
falling in perfect drops
into a plastic jar.

Paul Bennett

Red and Black and White

So we always keep the same hearts, though
our outer framework fails and shows the touch of time.
— Sarah Orne Jewett

I

The deep beech woods rings with the cry
of a pileated woodpecker in undulating flight,
possessive, electrifying, emotional,
and I think how Thoreau hungered
to find that great bird, hear it cry
its colors: red and black and white.
Once he found and heard the bird
I like to think Thoreau would have ascribed
red as the cry of a child from its heart,
black and white as the narration of an adult.
How he would have joined the two, I don't know,
although he named the end of enterprise *family.*

II

I never see or hear the pileated woodpecker
but I look back on a happy half century,
recalling that spring evening of instinctual vision
when I first saw Jeanne walking patterned bricks
leading from Chubb Library to college gateway;
my heart cried *red*: she's the one,
the only one, now or never!
A voice, not mine, came from my throat:
"Who are you, and where, when, how?"
Then I too spoke in *black and white*:
"I am an unknown, a nobody from nowhere;
I'd give anything—everything— to know you."

Appalachian Mettle

Mildred and Jim

Memory's tapestry comes in gold brocade:
he, dashing, dark, strong, intense;
she, fragile, fine-boned, reticent,
her face on elegant neck a helianthus
bending to him. Their natures, complex,
scarcely to be understood apart from the night
she discovered he did not measure up,
was terrified of heights, the dark, and fear itself.

I recall a summer visit to their house:
he paced and stomped the ground shouting
directions; she smiled, worked out a coil of rope,
lassoed the great overhanging oak, drew herself
aloft, clung, loosed the saw at her side,
cut and lowered the storm-torn limb
threatening to fall on their lives.

Hers became the courage of countless women
who accept the hand they are dealt
and play it to its earthy end, as she did
after his mid-life death, rearing seven children,
holding out body and work-worn hands to the
world, loving with the strength of ten.

Paul Bennett

Russell

An eighty-one-year-old heart falters and fails;
its owner writhes in pain, dies, and is buried.
I walk the woods at dusk hearing hardwood leaves
and pine needles shuffle under quick animal feet,
the fire-popping sound of a red deer leaping
breaking shoulder-high dead pine branches, white
flag flying, the silence of the woods returning,
settling in for the long, long night.

Dusk descends on the Gnaden High baseball
diamond; we hold a one run lead in the ninth, two
are out, a man on second, Wainwright's power
hitting third baseman at bat. Three balls, two strikes,
the pitch: the solid crunch of polished ash biting
horsehide, the long arc of white sphere to left field
where there is no fence, where a copper creek of
coal-mine drainage cuts left field from public road.

Carl Berkshire, our manager by whose side I sit,
groans: "There goes the game, the damned ball
game!" But wait: from out the shadows of left field
a ghost comes sailing, running from under his hat,
leaping the creek, red-hair flying. With gloved hand
up and out-stretched he nails the errant white sphere
and lands on the far side of the copper creek.

Amid frenzied applause, the baserunner crossing
home plate wilts, slams his hat in the dirt; the
batter, who is rounding first with arms up-raised,
sashays to the dugout. Carl Berkshire raises his
finger: "Thank God I played Russell E. as in *Red*,
had him lurking there in far left field."

27

Appalachian Mettle

Ralph

Outside the window three poison ivy leaves burn
like spilled blood in the setting October sun
reminding me ivy and bittersweet grow as one,
and he was both brother and father, bittersweet
gatherer, employer of last resort, tough but generous.

Born immune to poison oak and poison ivy
he said immunity could be taken on his say-so
and he said-so, and so it was, for my immunity
to poison oak and ivy is with me still.

As I grew I measured myself by his hands,
sleek, wiry, square, as powerful as vises.
I made nightmares of what might have been
long after the night he caught the armed thief
at cellar door, grabbed the 12-guage shotgun,
in instant of firing forced the barrel to the ground.

Memories raise nightmares and dreams we labor with
all the way to the grave: the blast of shotgun
and stench of gunpowder in gash of red clay;
those joyous days, months, years of our hunting,
trapping, aligning our lives to premises
that became promises, grew to principles.

He was and is my listener-confidant, stable
as the evening star though he died by suicide—
which I never understood, will never understand—
his chest gaping like earth itself, reeking of gunpowder.

Paul Bennett

Clyde

Carpenter, cabinet-maker, writer, he began
in his youth with a chicken house built
of used lumber. Hands leading eyes and mind
he found he could build almost anything:
clocks, cabinets, tables, chairs, desks,
boats, houses—work superbly whatever wood
declared itself right by taste that fixed
on the horizon of perfection he longed for
but could not reach.

Late in life, turning from wood to words
he polished facts to eloquence, fitted
thought to thought as grain to grain
in carpentry. Grounded in memory
his horizon of words led him and me
and a California visitor to the farm where,
sixty years after, we found the massive white mansion
abandoned, mouldering in the hungry ground,
its chicken house still standing, a thing of beauty.

Appalachian Mettle

Gene

Throughout the 1930 winter Gene made us believe
his tennis shoes shed the icy water we sloshed
through at the coal mine tipple where we dragged
gunny sacks gathering stray lumps, down the mucky
corn rows where we dragged gunny sacks
gleaning nubbins missed by the combine.

Gene was older, tougher, a survivor;
he knew what it was to go to bed hungry
and how to sleep three in a bed:
knew to place me with my shakes and shivers
in the middle, the one given to trots—Bob—
nearest the door. He said there should be
no secrets in a house and no place on earth
for those who hog the bed's single cover.

Paul Bennett

Hazel

Budding flower in a house of seven men,
born with brown eyes and hair, petal-soft hands,
she mastered jacks, roller skates, jumping rope,
rescued orphaned birds, dog-torn small animals,
and was taught she could measure men
by the world's most loving father.

With mother as model she married young,
moved south, rode the tractor beside her man,
did her housework on the side,
bore him two children, nurtured
and cared for the three of them
till the day he deserted her.

Long she studied herself, her house, her town,
the skittering sweet gum leaves, the powdery sand,
then with self-mocking smile she bought
three French poodles and made of her yard
a garden bright with annual flowers,
planted the town itself in marigolds.

Appalachian Mettle

Bob

Silver spoon striking antique China teacup
echoes cowbells from the long meadow
beside the Big Stillwater
near the town of Tippecanoe,
and I hear the desperate call
from Fort Lee before you went overseas,
sergeant commanding a Patton tank—
your call to me at Sheepshead Bay
praying we could get together,
but my C.O. denying me leave,
saying the Navy had need of me.

Had we got together there,
before the State made you a murderer,
would we have relived how little we knew of war,
how much we knew of green fields and orchards,
of the woods where we played our summer games
until time to go for the cows,
locating them by that distant silvery sound?

Trailing them while they quenched their thirst
and tramped through the fragrant mint,
hooves clean-washed, as beautiful as eyes,
into the ensilaged-scented barn,
the click of cow ties, thump of stantion oak
polished to glaze by eager leather necks;
how we snatched our milking stools, settled
our heads in nooks of brown and white flanks,
sweat on our heads smelling of mint,
hands folding, pulling down the frothy white
into pails between legs, shooting off a jet

Paul Bennett

now and then to a leg-caressing, meowing cat.
Had we met at Fort Lee or Sheepshead Bay
would we have recalled the milking done,
milk strained into white and brown crocks,
crocks set in the springhouse to cool
while we raced on fleet barefeet
carrying our go-to-town clothes,
our towels and slivers of soap
to our bathing spot by the willowed pool?

Silver striking antique China echoes
fifty years and more—before the war,
before the State made you a murderer,
before your chest bore many medals,
before war made you an alcoholic,
before you yourself were found murdered,
before ever I beheld the ancient Buick
with its bloodstained front seat,
its window drilled by a thirty-eight,
before my conversation with the undertaker,
with the coroner, with the sheriff,
before I was shown the pictures of you
lying on the front seat in a pool of blood.

Had you and I got together in New Jersey or New York
would we have told how we bathed
and dressed in our go-to-town clothes
and came by to pick up Aunt Sarah's wicker basket
with its three pound-prints of fresh-churned butter—
each bearing its sprig of green mint—
to deliver to three needy families
in the town of Tippecanoe
down on the Big Stillwater?

Appalachian Mettle

Where Rivers Meet

Spring

Hand-in-hand he and she walked riverbank
where the Muskingum meets the Ohio;
long and soft they talked, as lovers will,
of a world on whirl, men and women estranged,
and whether perhaps they lucked out
by being in Marietta on the Ohio,
where by premise they might perceive
what lay upstream of blue river bridge
that time uncoiling would bring to them.

Summer

When sunny river bore but an empty barge
and his hands grew hot to hold her close
in all her wanton willowness,
she said: "Don't fret. You and I will go to bed
when you, like this ground mole at our feet,
wander at will beneath the earth."

He let go her hand, exclaiming: "God,
how fair you are, what games you play!"

Seizing his hand, pressing it to her breast,
she said: "You failed the test. Could you, dear,
have become a spelunker of caves,
a West Virginia coal miner? I'll give you
one more challenge, one more chance."

Paul Bennett

Fall

"I hear you," he said. "I treasure your every word
and so I ask: Will you marry me?"

"Of course," she said. "I wouldn't be here
if I wouldn't." She paused. "But one thing more:
I will only marry you—lawyerly repeat—
only marry you the day you walk on water."

"Easy," he said. "Meet me in moonlit September
where we swim in the Muskingum, where water maple
holds our diving rope. I'll prove to you
I can walk on water naked as the day I was born."

"Unfair," she said. "No ropes allowed, but I promise
I will marry you the day you walk on water."

Winter

"Hm—mm," he said. "You do make life difficult—
but interesting. Meet me at Marietta's Lafayette Hotel
for lunch on my birthday in January."

War came on December 7, and she called to ask,
"Will you marry me? I'm enroute to Marietta."

He laughed. "I once heard a wise woman say,
'I wouldn't be here if I wouldn't.'"

P.S. He and she met for lunch at the Lafayette,
    then walked on ice at the river's edge.

Part II

Paul Bennett

Tracking Big Game in Ohio

Through five-year-old eyes he beheld
the red brick bell tower of the school
aflutter with legions of pigeons,
and so he had reason to believe his brother
who told him the second floor hallway
teemed with wild animals
that man had found a way to tame:
"Deer, elk, moose—they're all there," he said,
"and if you go Indian you'll get close enough
to touch their ears and their antlers."

In early dusk he climbed the steep
concrete steps, silently swung the heavy door,
crossed the shadowy hall, and waited,
hoping to catch the stomp of hoofs,
the slap-slap shaking down of hairy coats,
the warm sound of animals chewing;
as he crept up the second set of stairs
his head rang loud with his breathing
and in the summery dark he felt for
and found the light switch.

The blaze of light revealed
four deer, three elk, and two moose,
and under each antlered head a plaque
naming the hunter and date of his kill.
Turning out the light he made his way
back down the grooved ladders of oak,
down the steep steps of concrete,
vowing he would tell his brother
he had found the wild animals,
had felt their sinewy flanks and furry tails.

Appalachian Mettle

Essay: On Schools

Between the white brick and our house
there was the older school
where I stopped evenings enroute:
the ancient butcher above his block
swinging a cleaver in his quaking fist,
sawdust off the floor on his apron,
shreds of tobacco waxy on his lips.

Neat black bloodstains here and there,
liquid specials dripped on windows,
the sun creeping across the floor,
peanuts in a bowl, the checkerboard,
the stacked men awaiting first move,
soft heat of lights and livers of calves,
smoke of flesh, smell verging on vinegar.

And all I learned there,
where I could never out stare
the dying red eye of a Rhode Island rooster.

Paul Bennett

On Reforming Education

Led by Bennett and Bloom professional educators
prate, urging return to formal learning which
yielded the perfection they demonstrate.
Because it cannot come again
I explain a little history lesson of 1928
in an Ohio town: our second grade class
was visited now and then by a Civil War veteran,
an eighty-four-year old self-appointed school
inspector who wore a Union blue overcoat, each
pocket loaded with a sack of white peppermint or
pink wintergreen lozenges.

When our turn came we each read as well as we
could and were invited to reach into a pocket for a
lozenge. What we liked most was that every reader
won, even we klutzes of the class, and no one knew
beforehand whether right or left pocket
held the favorite pink wintergreens—
bags flew from pocket to pocket while we read.

At recess we got to hear the real Civil War:
how snowy mud turned Camp Yorktown into
"Camp Misery," how dusty-hot blood-sticky the
grass at Bull Run, how sickening the stench of
animals and men in The Wilderness; and we got to
see and lift the heavy Belgian rifle, "My
government's gift in 1862 to start the new year—
something fit and proper in time of war, I reckon,
but I wish to God I'd never held it in my hand."

Appalachian Mettle

A Teacher Remembered
(For Ralph W. Johnson)

A seventh grade teacher of mathematics
whose middle initial stood for *Wonderful*,
he was a bear of a man, his face and neck
branded by a wine birthmark
which one has difficulty remembering,
although he told us time and again
math was itself a precise and finite way
of seeing, believing, remembering.

The first day of class we stood
to the right of our desks joining hands
to say the multiplication tables
to the strength of twelve, and then practiced,
his finger pointing to each of us,
ways to count to one hundred by twos,
by fives, by tens, and by his swinging
"Ten, ten, double ten, forty-five, fifteen!"
Raising his hand he silenced us and mused:
"Is there not a quicker way?"
Pierce Grabling, our morning star, responded:
"Maybe fifty-fifty?" Ralph W. nodded:
"Right! Right makes might! and you,
my boy, receive a perfect grade: one hundred."

The day he gave us our last math test
we stood in what had become a ritual
and passed to the right of our desks,
each an integer—"integer vitae," he murmured—
to form a line, become a survey chain

Paul Bennett

to shape and fix in memory
a rectangle, a square, a perimeter,
varieties of triangles,
a circle, a circumference, a diameter.

From the circle we walked past his desk
on which he had laid out the contents
of all its drawers: a compass; two rulers,
his green grade book, a gum eraser,
a bouquet of rubber bands, a stack of index cards,
two bottles of ink, blue and red,
a black fountain pen with gold band,
five No. 2 yellow pencils, a first aid kit,
seven confiscated penknives, one set of jacks,
three marbles, and the blue box
of California figs he sucked on
when we returned "in orderly fashion, no crawling over,
ladies are ladies, gentlemen, gentlemen,"
to our desks to list and number
as much as we could remember.

Appalachian Mettle

Winter Flood

On the railroad bridge we stood
in wind-driven snow
above pounding brown current
that carried an ice floe
bearing a gaunt gray mare and foal;
the floe swept against the bridge pier, held,
then broke.

Amid grinding ice the white-eyed mare
turned, took in the lessened ice floe,
nudged her foal to its center,
then backed into the flood,
leaving a shivering monument
to ride the diminished floe
to shore.

Softly I sang my mother's name.

Paul Bennett

A Heave-Ho Horseman

He once named himself a heave-ho horseman
born after his time and left-handed to boot.
His left-handed deftness enabled him to become
the best corn-husker in the State of Ohio
when corn husking was still an art and a calling.
His left-handed thinking destroyed his marriage
but earned him two patents,
one for a mar-less nail puller,
the second for a clinching automobile tire
when tires were given to flying off their rims.

To get to his house you had to cross Laurel Creek,
which you did by fording or by footlog—
privacy before bridges. On his side of Laurel Creek
you got to meet his black stallion Prince
who seldom lost a stake race
and whose thinking he honored:
"Two minds are better than one," he said
"even if one is a persnickety Perissodactyla;
Prince says we do not go to town today."—
this on those days when he was unable to catch Prince
by sorgum-laced oats or human stratagem.

Appalachian Mettle

Team Logging

Before ever they began their felling
experienced sawyers walked a wood
calculating how it might saw out:
board feet of poplar, oak, maple, gum—
trees cluster in clans like men and women.

At sunrise of the second day
the logger arrived with his powerful team—
sorrels and he seemed carved from a red oak log.
Dragging doubletree and long log chain
they tip-toed the narrow entry path
past ferns, violets, crows' feet, and
May apple's green elephant ears
attuned to the whispering sun;
they crashed the diamond-studded spider's gate
to where in leafy sod the downed logs lay.

Gee-hawed among the stumps, the sorrels
leaned to their harness, haunches digging,
set logs gliding: in deep wood's bleeding
logs slid down to the hungry saw.
Hour after hour, day after day
sorrels and logger worked the wooded hill,
polished to silver the great log chain.

Trusting horse sense and his own quick feet
in the deep wood the logger never once
knotted his lines—let the reins trail free
lest they catch, and snap his back or neck.
But when the day's work was done

he unhitched the doubletree and chain,
whipped the reins into a knot and lolled back,
giving the sorrels their homing heads;
they whistled him down to the willowed creek
and where the sparkling minnows ran, muzzled deep.

Appalachian Mettle

Appalachian Man
(For Russell Decker)

Burdened by a hill-country
run-of-the-mine education,
more given to observing
and listening than speaking,
he spent a lifetime
looking after his mother and father,
doing those home-keeping tasks
most of us find ways to ignore.

When his parents died
he sought out and married
an eighty-year-old widow
who needed a man
about the house, someone
to chop stove wood, tend
the fires, shovel snow,
see after the animals.

Using his life's savings
he sent his wife's granddaughters
off to college, launched them in professional
careers, explaining that diamonds differ
from common coal, and after
a warm spring rain
one should search out the morel.

Paul Bennett

Stuck on Open
(For Karl Zimmermann)

Built like a professional football tackle, he loomed
larger than life all those Depression years
of our growing up in that Tuscarawas River town
where we heard his deep voice proclaim
he had ridden into town on the spring flood
and ended up owning rich river bottom land
where receding flood waters deposited him.

A meticulous gardener, barefoot and barefisted,
he smiled as he said: "A nobody could fill my
shoes." He worked alongside our crew of twenty,
raising acres of rhubarb, asparagus, strawberries,
sweet corn, melons, tomatoes, spinach—produce
enough to keep his truck on the road to Pittsburgh
six nights a week all summer long.

By his example, hoe in hand, he taught us
gardening, women, and generosity. So many times
I heard it, I close my eyes and hear it now, his
gravel voice turned tender: "That is a problem; I'll
have to see what the *little woman* thinks." And I see
her still: a *little woman* who filled completely the
doorway of their white farm house.

When poverty and winter winds froze our breaths
and Depression hunger gnawed our bones, he drove
his truck to haul our coal. With him you could order
half a ton of coal and know he'd deliver a ham or
side of bacon and a five ton load, saying: "You pay
for the half ton you ordered; that crazy mine's
loading chute stuck on open."

Appalachian Mettle

Cy Young as Poet

Strong the sun that October afternoon
Ralph, Bob and I drove Ralph's green Chrysler
down country roads west of Gilmore
gathering bittersweet to haul to florists
in Pittsburgh and Cleveland. Cashing in
on our immunity to poison ivy
we untangled great ropes of gold bittersweet
from fences and trees, from poison ivy and Virginia
Creeper whose three and five leaves glowed
vermilion glazed in the sun's fiery kiln.

We cut and gathered and talked family
and history, the luck of finding a living name.
Bob and I laughed when Ralph told of General U.S.
Grant (*U*nconditional *S*urrender Grant after Fort
Donelson), named at birth Hyram Ulysses Grant,
nominated to West Point as Ulysses Simpson Grant
(*Simpson* being his mother's maiden name),
how Grant changed his name, officially and legally,
once he saw the advantage of being able to label his
trunk bound for West Point U.S.G. rather than the
mawkish H.U.G.

We talked bittersweet and baseball, and Ralph
told us we stood that moment within a stone's throw
of the farm of his friend Denton True Young,
baseball's most enduring pitcher, perhaps its
greatest, who had pitched over nine hundred games,
won more than five hundred, and how he—Denton
True Young—became "Cy" the afternoon he tried
out for the big leagues in Canton. The catcher,

unable to hold Denton True Young's fast pitch,
permitted passed ball after passed ball, balls
that hit the wooden backstop, leaving it
as though shattered by a Young cyclone.

The sun finally sinking, a cool dusk descending,
Ralph's old Chrysler's back seat loaded like a tub
of gold grapes bound for the winery,
we called it a day, then drove by and stopped
at Cy Young's farm. Ralph wanted to thank Cy
for the bittersweet we'd gathered on his place;
Bob and I wanted to hear baseball, catch
the splat of tobacco juice, the rattle of fast balls
riddling barn planks, for Ralph had told us
Cy learned to control his speed pitch by hurling
green walnuts in fall, frozen horse biscuits in winter
at a worn horse collar hung on the gray barn side.

We passed a farm house and stopped at the barn
beyondwhere Ralph led Bob and me to a bear of a
man clad in denim, gargantuan in the shadows
cast by his flickering chore lantern. His voice
surprised us—high and soft—as he talked weather,
a good corn crop, his having harvested three
cuttings of clover hay from two hilltop fields, and a
fine tree of persimmons waiting for the frost if only
the possums would leave them alone. Bob and I
waited for the pitcher to emerge from the bullpen
as the talk turned to cattle and Cy Young said he
was likely to lose a Hereford Calf named "Roger"
to a bad case of cattle scours.
"Calves find a way to die of diarrhea," Ralph said,

"but sometimes they'll respond to a handful of bran
and a good teaspoon of salt in their milk."
"Thanks. I'll try that," Cy said as we prepared to
leave. Bob could control himself no longer.
"Your calf named Rogers," he asked, "is his last
name Hornsby by any chance?" Cy Young clapped
his hands and smiled. "Rogers Hornsby—there's a
name! If I'd named him that, he'd live, I'll bet."
He turned to Ralph and winked, but spoke to Bob:
"If he shows real spunk I'll call him Ty—
Cy's Ty Cobb! Try that for size!"

Paul Bennett

Coyote

He grew up at home with animals, rocks, trees,
and when at school we were asked to choose
what we would want to be
he became a coyote. He knew
how to find and run down small game,
how the wind rose in the night sky,
how water made its way through rocks
and where it could be found in cold pools.

Having him for friend was like being free
to choose your own brother; with him
on your side you could play any ball game
with one less player. Nobody I knew
could keep up with him in running:
he'd let you set the start and finish lines,
you'd start ahead but he'd leave you behind.

When war came most of us chose the Navy;
he became a paratrooper and was first overseas.
Years later one who was with him when he died
told me how his pulsing legs carried him
ahead of all others down cobbled German streets,
how he charged, charged, charged,
and took the bullets in his stride
till they took the top off his head.

Appalachian Mettle

Last Meeting with "Pedo"
(For Earl B. Crites, 1921 - 1991)

Rough-hewn, bearing our share of time's claw
marks, retired mason, retired teacher, he and I sit
side by side at Gnaden High's reunion banquet
ignoring the amplified drone of a hired humorist
who thinks himself Bob Hope, trying as best we can
to bridge more than half a century. We speak
of girls, baseball, basketball, track,
classes and study halls, and he reminds me
how often we combined our shaky hold
on math, chemistry, history, English
to see each other cross a flower-wreathed stage.

We replay our World War II roles:
he a B-24 pilot, I a landing ship navigator.
He relives a fellow pilot's death:
a nightmare harvest-moon flight into Germany,
his squadron caught in a cauldron of flak
the moment they cross the coast. His plane
bracketed, bucking, but unscathed;
his friend's plane hit, blasted, set afire,
the crew killed save three, radioman, bombardier,
pilot friend.

In mind's eye he sees through blood pink haze
his friend's guages go haywire, altimeter spinning,
overhears once more the last message:
"Unload bombs on nearest lights, head
for North Sea." He sees bombs lift high
what has to be an occupied village school,

Paul Bennett

the rising rubble dust, and he escorts his friend
all the way down to a watery grave.

He tells how, back from the war, he becomes
a master mason, spends a lifetime building
restaurants, churches, banks, schools—
making stones fill gaps in space, bricks arch
over open space, a symphony by trowel,
a life that goes to make stone and mortar stay,
"Maybe a way to strike a balance." He clears his throat.

I nod, remembering "Pedo" riding out
of Cherry Street's early morning fog,
pedaling his creaking bicycle, right pedal missing,
stopping to lean on our cement front porch,
call for me, hitch his pants, readying himself
to ride the two of us to Karl Zimmermann's farm,
where we happily pick strawberries all day long
for the going wage of one cent per quart.

Appalachian Mettle

A Hardware Clerk
(For Ida C.)

Tall, willow-quick, with squirrel bright eyes,
her fame firm-set on courage in crisis
(last person to cross the collapsing wagon bridge
before the flooding Tuscarawas River
swept it away), she lived out her long life
in the dim shadows of Campbell's Hardware
as if wedded to rows of copper miner's lamps,
the acrid smell of carbide and blasting powder.

Suitors whom she rejected accused her
of being sexually drawn to guns and pick-axes;
she showed little patience with these macho men
who shoulder-rolled their sleeves year 'round.
When told they were as tough as ten-penny nails,
she said: "It's easy to take size for substance,
a six-penny nail is as tough as a
twenty-penny spike—
truly tough nails come case hardened."

She knew by heart the price of every item
in the store, how to cut glass, repair
most machinery, how to wire a house, set
a charge of dynamite. Farmers, miners,
plumbers, electricians said:
"When things don't work, ask Ida."
And we barefoot boys in town knew
we could go to her with one thin dime
and get three fishhooks of finest Swedish steel.

Paul Bennett

Lenthiel H. Downs on Earth
(1915 - 1996)

Forget the thousands he taught,
forget the audiences he awed,
still he stands head high on the premise of facts
conversing with Joyce, Mann, Proust, Faulkner,
Welty with jocoserious intent. A democrat,
of all people, for all people,
celebrant of time and place
he met our mandate for greatness: he introduced us
to facts, not self, and made all of us
the richer for the literature he read.

Old friend, you and I and our wives stand on
riverbank before the setting sun shining on Black
Hand Gorge and you speak biblical knowledge with
wit too sharp for any but a subtle mind: "That man
who would say *man shall have dominion here*
should be cut down to his knees in prayer."

The Two Worlds of Banty Hutton

He lived alone on a hill above our town,
enduring fixture on a front porch
of clay-stained timbers scrounged
from the abandoned Daisy Mine tipple.

When my brother Ralph and I visited him
he was eager to debate taxes,
war, religion, and the New Deal
for which Ralph had become a partisan.

I carried away from gray-timbered porch
memories of the sun setting, yellow jackets
clustered in drunken clouds above
fragrant piles of transparent apples;

gamecocks fighting for roosting space
on swaying apple limbs; and Banty Hutton,
raising his finger, cocking his head,
and stepping to the edge of the porch

to reverently identify by name
and pedigree each of five long-dead hounds
that would forever be running
the shadowy red and gray foxes.

Paul Bennett

Flyways

Our mysterious mythic flyways—
East Coast, Mid-Continent, Far West—
honor Daedalus and son Icarus,
feature pools of polished silver
graced with sun and water's splendor,
way stations of food, drink, and rest
for waterfowl and land birds.

Artificial suns light another maze
of flyways, shared by moths and men.
Intricate as a labyrinth, east to west,
north to south, these flyways draw
crows and soaring birds that circle
to feed on roadkills, on every creature
that dies and lies still.

Part III

Paul Bennett

The Black Stone
(For Gene)

Finite, yet infinite,
the black stone fills my hand
with Gulf of Mexico's warmth,
sun wedded to water, water to stone
more textured than obsidian,
worked into seamless beauty
in moon's great mill.

Fitting to fullness
the black stone warms my hand
like the fist of my Floridian brother
when he lay in his hospital bed,
ballasted with the weight of death,
his hard life polished smooth
by time's dark waves.

Appalachian Mettle

Third Man in the Ring: Arthur Donovan

I

During the Depression years in Ohio
our audience, cows; pasture pennyroyal our laurel,
my brother, a professional, taught me to box—
and he and I hunched at our hiccuping radio
whenever the Brown Bomber in 8-oz gloves
stalked his prey under Art Donovan's judicious eye.
Wherever the fight—New York, St. Louis,
Detroit—*his* presence certified its integrity,
the sway of Marquis of Queensberry's rules,
and my brother and I could have believed
he had refereed the Olympic Games in 686 B.C.

II

During the war, at Sheepshead Bay Training Sta-
tion, Art Donovan strode into my life: at fifty-two
he toed the canvas-floored twenty-foot square ring
parrying blows and riding the ropes like an Olym-
pian, helping us glory-mad sailors master ropes and
canvas to please the gods of the sea. And I could
believe the scuttlebutt prevailing on base:
that he had taught President Teddy Roosevelt to
box, had entered the White House by side door
but had come and gone by the front.

Our taped fists in hot gloves, we heard him state:
"When I say 'break,' you break; when I say 'stop,'
you stop; when I say 'box,' you box. In event of a

knockdown you withdraw to the farther neutral corner.
Now go back to your corners and come out fighting." In
the station messhall I heard him explain to officers and
their wives over a dinner of lamb: "A referee has to see
every blow that's struck
but never get in either boxer's way—
he's got to know for sure who wins the fight."

III

The New York *Times* told us Art Donovan
died in 1980 at the generous age of eighty-nine.
Those of us who cared for him knew this
to be a second death. He died in 1946
after a night on the town with a friend,
in a quarrel over who got to pay the taxi bill:
a blow to the jaw caught his friend and he fell,
his head bursting like a melon on concrete curb.
Later, with tears in his eyes, Art Donovan said:
"I don't know what happened—he was my best friend."

Appalachian Mettle

Little Man, Standing Tall

How do you deal with the cursing man
walking on his heels toward the supermarket door,
who suddenly slaps his cringing daughter
and begins to beat his cowering wife? Is it fair
to seize a nearby shopping cart and
accidentally wheel it into his behind?

And if you do, are you prepared to apologize,
to have him transfer his anger to you
and in a mounting voice slander your mother?
If seeing you thrust your hands in your pockets
he judges you to be a coward, and insists—
for the world to hear—on the right
to meet you in the parking lot?

Would it be fair to explain to him—
if *he* could be got to listen—
that you do not believe in fighting
although you grew up where one fought or died,
that you sparred regularly with your brother,
a professional fighter, and in the Navy went six
rounds with New England's Golden Gloves Middle-
weight champ, that you had this very morning
skipped rope and worked out with the shadow of
your brother?

But you lock your fists in your pockets,
mouth humble pie, and watch with joy
the little man strut off boasting
to wife and daughter and crowd

how he would have kicked that old geezer's ass
all over the god-damned parking lot.

Later, as luck would have it, you find
the little man, standing tall, waiting for you
at the checkout counter. Again he curses you
while wife and daughter look on with sweet
understanding, and so you lower your head and
softly say: "I'm sorry. Bless you, bless you,"
meaning it, meaning every word of it.

Appalachian Mettle

Some Spirited Men

When the moon is full as it is tonight
I remember my brother Ralph who held
the Depression world in his large fist:
undefeated as a professional fighter, floor foreman
of a steel mill in Weirton, West Virginia,
avid follower of Joe Louis in the ring,
Ernest Hemingway in the library.

Worshipper of natural law,
how was he to foresee that three thugs,
intent on robbery, would blackjack him
from behind, shatter his skull, write *fini*
to his dreams of a ring career,
his fine judgment in working men and steel?

The Methodist minister said: "Man proposes,
God disposes," but Ralph cried, "Foul!" Retreating
to a farm he gained renown as a gatherer of bitter-
sweet, October's vine-moored golden globes
that he deleafed, bunched, and delivered
to florists in Cleveland, Columbus, Pittsburgh.

Some spirited men refuse to become guinea pigs;
Ralph was such a man. Friends, neighbors, family
set the trap, made him feel he had failed.
In the full-moon light he loaded his 12-guage,
made sure it was cocked, ready to fire,
pressed to his chest its blue-steel wedding band
and sent his finger to the trigger.

Paul Bennett

The Small Animal

I am the small animal
clinging to your screen door
when you rush to it at 2 a.m.
after your dog's uproar.

Mine is the broken chest
ripped out at shoulder
where bloodied lung shows;
mine the urine spilled down
the screen and held there
like honey to the light.

Mine is the heart
whose erratic explosions
give motion to the door
as though I would close it
against your leaping dog
or open it to you.

Already my body vermin know
I smell of death;
they are dropping
one by one to come to you.

Appalachian Mettle

Walnut Girl

You are all walnut, girl,
your essence I recall
from my youth as a slab-bearer
in an Ohio mill.

I lean to you now,
weeping against a college wall,
as if walls were made
for meanings biblical.

I taste your tears,
touch your leaves, last to come,
first to go, changing sunlight
to flesh and shadow.

Subtle of grain, root wild,
we share pasts that stain,
stains that sting. Our fate
is written in cold rain.

Paul Bennett

By Lantern

By lantern
in the winter night
the breeched calf
is turned.

From the womb
dropped on mottled snow,
sheltered from death
only by quick hands
stained in the fight.

Intimate as breath
life grows impertinent:
a steel-file tongue
rasps your brow.

Appalachian Mettle

A Neighborly Visit

The kind May sun corrected my heavy hand
by making the garden hose spray a rainbow,
and while I stood by, dumbfounded,
a hummingbird paused in midair,
then alighted on dark earth and bathed:

Carefully cleansed each fine feathered wing,
his iridescent hackles, his crimson crown,
and with long ivory bill, new washed,
sipped of the mist. Thirst-quenched
he sped off to a walnut limb.

There he preened and dried himself
and eyed the sun in blue space, then
launched himself to a nearby beech
that swung his mate and their two white eggs
in a hammock spun of spider web.

Paul Bennett

The Duchess Pear

Rose family rose
peachy with down
its fragrance virginal
the pear in bloom
takes the female form.

Its stigma sticky
with bee-borne pollen
the ovary swells
becomes woman shaped
a sun-orbiting star.

Sheathed in gold sheen
it welcomes
the laying on of hands
the mouthing of its fine grained flesh.

But once beholding
a Duchess pear
any male is stung by man's desire
to reach the moon.

Appalachian Mettle

Sweet Cherries

How do you keep birds
from eating all your cherries?
Cherry-eating birds are friends,
They pick those branches
I'd break my neck to reach.
How do you keep birds
from eating all your cherries?
I grow so many cherries
birds can't eat them all.

Sweet cherries honor history:
Windsor, Royal Ann, Napoleon,
Tartarian, Seneca, Bing,
Kansas City—the list runs on,
and we experience on our tongue
what every cherry picker knows
in language of the street:
a cherry is precious flesh.

When I wish to close on life
I climb a great sweet cherry tree
in light rain and summer lightning
to pick the plump fruit by mouth.
Aloft I am in the presence of brothers
who years ago climbed with me:
we are animals on generous limbs
and death is a distant rumor.

Paul Bennett

Surgeon to Trees

As surgeon to trees
I have removed much deadwood
I would otherwise be carrying,
I have learned to cut close and neat,
to keep a wound clean
for proper healing. I have performed
transfusions from rainbows,
and in the triangular relation
of sun, moisture, and my eye
I have seen that more depends
upon my view of others
than upon their view of me.

Appalachian Mettle

Grapes

Having spent years learning how grapes grow,
still I am stopped in this vineyard
where a forty-year-old Concord quivers
under a windless April sky,
stretches forth tendrils like fingers,
lending a handhold, a steadying grip,
to a struggling Himrod vine.

Delicate blossoms of white tatting
perfume this green hillside,
transporting me to B.C. Italy
where I hear an old Roman proclaim:
"If one be wise, he will retire to a vineyard,
and if one finds a friend he can trust,
he will guard that friend with his life."

Paul Bennett

The Deer at Middleton

The poet came to us by air,
out of France via New York City,
bearing three pieces of luggage
and the heaviest of baggage:
never having known her father
apart from his having been
her mother's parish priest.

At Middleton Guest House she found
rural Ohio green and real.
I showed her to her second floor room,
stowed her luggage, and crossed the room
to raise the shades. What I beheld
caused my heart to leap; without speaking
I beckoned to her and pointed:

Emerging from woods on green lawn
came eleven deer on parade—
does, fawns, and antlered buck—
gracefully ambling toward farm pond.
She grew wide-eyed as a child,
her face blooming and then her voice:
"Father, father! Thank you, thank you."

Part IV

Paul Bennett

The Ravenous Bed

When you arrive you will find
a young woman making a bed;
she will nod casually and say:
"I did not expect you today
but you are welcome. I will add
an extra pillow; we can push the bed
to the wall. There will be space
(she raises her arms to you),
there will be room for you.
Many have lain here before you,
many will lie here after you,
but I was keeping this space for you."

As you sleep you will trade
your body's cold for her body's warmth.
In her arms you will awaken
to find gold glints in her hair,
a secret smile upon her lips,
and if her eyes are hidden
by her hair as in a mist,
you still will breathe the musk
of your own begetting, you will feel
your own blood drumming, pushing
you toward the everlasting sun
after so much darkness, so much cold.

Appalachian Mettle

On Making Love

I

In lily script
a lady wrote:
I will make love
to you, oh world,
tomorrow
when the apricots bloom.

On apricot bough
a brown bird sings;
pink buds unfold,
incandescent,
virginal.

II

From afar
another eye
embraces telescopic sight,
another finger calculates.
We hear the plunk
of lead on flesh.

Staring with dull eyes
into dead eyes
we surprise a world
sterile, blank.
Our tongues engage
in salty rape.

Paul Bennett

III

On apricot bough
a brown bird sings:
three deaths in one—
what then, what then?
After cerise sunrise
and saline spring
what sky distills
the growing rain?

We are not Christs
immaculate,
but tortured men,
enthralled by sun,
a hand that moves,
a head that always
hangs behind.

IV

One man said:
today I lived,
I caressed roots,
dug the hole,
prepared topsoil,
set the tree,
filled the hole,
worked out air,
pruned the tree,
and watered it.

Appalachian Mettle

V

On apricot bough
a brown bird sings:
three deaths in one,
what then, what then?

Impelled to kill,
to have and get,
to cultivate
a fulsome gut,
we revere
the lily script.

VI

Our mirrors give back
our bloodshot eyes
of yesterday.

On apricot bough
a brown bird sings:
I make love to you,
Oh World, today.

Paul Bennett

Canoeing

At a lecture
detailing the difference
between consumable writing
and literature
I kept wondering
how many patient men
have found stars
in dark wells?

Knowing you are
in another's arms
I remember how
I stood on my arms,
your face beneath me
unbelievably beautiful.

That I did not know
the J-stroke did not matter,
our canoe snaked
through the fast water,
through lakes like long grass,
hills, sunlit clouds;
your mouth rounded
with O's of pleasure.

Appalachian Mettle

On Carolinian Sand

Constant, fluid, the great heart pumps
dimensions of being, time-telling tide;
above and behind it all the moon,
behind the moon the sun, behind
the sun the all—or none.
On firm Carolinian sand
to the next fishing pier
it is 2.4 measured miles, certified
by automobile meter and tired feet.

The woman and I walk and talk,
she fresh from her northern home,
I from an inland conference
where there was much discussion
of what we had done, might do:
"Having conquered Everest and the moon
we must go on to master other worlds."
Our thoughts meander to this question:
does the Atlantic know it is conquered
when touched by intruding toe?

Although the coast is clear
as far as two pairs of eyes can see
ghostly ships fester on the grey horizon
plow into view and disappear—
on the pooled shore sanderlings run,
downwind swoops a disgruntled gull,
far off the sea is steady
as a pane of glass, but
from the shoreline to our rear

Paul Bennett

the owner of an Olympian swimming pool
curses out invading kids.

We walk and talk
of the setting sun that is not setting,
of Hera and Zeus on Olympus
and their happy lovers' quarrel:
whether male or female
took most pleasure from the act of love.
Teiresias, who had lived as man,
is made woman to ascertain the truth;
his verdict uttered, Hera struck him blind,
for what we know we cannot see.
Behind us a cluster of men and women
mouth certainties they live by in accents
borrowed from a foster mother's African tongue.

The woman and I stroll past our pier,
wondering how different our lives would be
if we understood the stroking of the sun
or one grain of sand on this wide beach,
which we do not, which we cannot.
At our feet a wee spider crab,
having seized an empty snail shell for house,
moves with the tide, comes and goes with it,
making a home on the roving wave.

Appalachian Mettle

One Word

In a strange town
after sixteen years
bits and pieces
like melons gather flavor:
small of your back,
a rabbit's tail
never seen by you;
sky's fleece,
heart's haven;
your face and eyes
night lights;
your hair—
my fingers touch
where thoughts begin;
against your lips
the crook of my tongue
unfolds one word.

Paul Bennett

The Tuscarawas River

Forever the same but different daily,
human in many ways, you ran
to tell us we too were interlopers
on the land, brief onlookers only.

Secretive in depths that hosted death
still you were our friend; irate or placid
you kept all values fluid, your reality
more humane than breath-stopping earth.

In your presence we found truth alive and well
and all walked naked: the priest revealed
his woman's body, the conductor his workman's
arms and legs, the minister his maggoty mind.

And I myself stood stark upon your bank
gazing on two New Straitsville girls
lying prone in John Zimmermann's canoe,
who sat bolt upright to behold male genitals.

Appalachian Mettle

Pilot Mountain

I wanted the mountain to become a part of
me so that I might become a part of it.
— Harry Truman, Botanist

I

Hidden by leafy panoply the trail
encircles North Carolina's Pilot Mountain
as though all life went there, on two legs or four,
treading time to find the safest path.
Jeanne and I, returning to Ohio
from driving parents south for the winter,
walk the sandy watercourse to a granite table
where dissected pine cones tell us
squirrels beat us to the morning sun,
enjoyed a leisurely breakfast.
Beside the trail a sign proclaims:
"No rock climbing at the pinnacle,"
to which Jeanne responds: "Thinking
required at every level."

II

It is not our tool-shaping hands
nor our early awareness of death
that sets us apart, though granite
we hold on to could read gravestone.
We move as once we climbed college hill
tips of fingers caressing breast and chest,
afternoon becoming dusk, a fine rain falling;
our eyes large from reading books and love
we pause to ponder raccoon prints in mud

Paul Bennett

beside the college walk. No other marks—
there need be none—guided us then,
guide us now, where we cling
and peer easterly farther than eye can see.

III

To name what we behold when *is* becomes *was*
gives life a long face: gone
all that great swampland, fragile, fertile wetland
stretching from New Jersey to Florida,
pinelands to Everglades,
gone the mating
of sky-sea-land in sustaining harmony,
and, farther south, the singing rainforest
that begot and fed the pristine Amazon. This
and the blue planet earth, sickened and enfeebled
by man; all life set at hazard, for man,
of all creatures, has the power to alter radically
his world, and does so perpetually
by taking dominion everywhere.

IV

Clinging to rock face, Jeanne turns her face
to me, her far-seeing grey eyes, her bright look
of knowing and caring. Smiling, without speaking,
she shakes her head and steps down. I follow, pointing
with tool-shaping hands outstretched:
she ducks the eye blink shadow of vulture
circling overhead. We laugh, and speak of family:
two sons will be our share, our way to limit use,
name it harm to what is ours to hold briefly,
an Ohio hillside farm, the slight bit we can do
to repair what man has torn asunder.

Appalachian Mettle

In Ancient Rite

On a blustery March day they drove
for one last time to their wooded acreage:
there, tracking the sun, avoiding harsh winds
they followed a grassed-over creek bed
that circled a knoll through a stand of hardwoods—
walnuts, maples, beeches, oaks—
he walking ahead, she going ever slower
just to allow him once more the lead.

He disappeared around a slight bend,
then hurried back: Moses from the mountain,
his eyes on fire, finger to his lips,
his right hand laying down *quiet*.
He waited as she tiptoed to him,
and silent as shades they moved forward.

At eye-height she saw what he had seen:
a fawn curled asleep in sun-trapping hollow
at foot of an oak. As one they crept
up the bank to stand within arm's reach,
studying, storing details of mottled coat
in its rhythmic, slight rise and fall,
dimpled black nose resting on bent foreleg,
black hoofs shining as though carved of flint.

In ancient rite she knelt and touched
an ear that felt like mullein leaf:
the fawn, dreaming of flies perhaps,
twitched the ear but slept on,
slept on as they caressed the warm flank
where a few guard hairs glowed cornelian.

Paul Bennett

At last they stood, exchanged glances, smiles,
and backed away. Descending the embankment
she whispered: "Where would the doe be?"
"Somewhere close, within hearing, guarding it,
probably watching us even at this moment."
Their hands before them as if bearing gifts
they followed the dry creek bed,
making their way, long way round, to the car.

Appalachian Mettle

A Valentine for Jeanne

Once again I tramp the damp loam
with you, seeking five-fingered leaves,
the slight umbels, green and white,
the red berries, the man-shaped roots.

Dug and dried over winter, they lay
their faint lickerish on my tongue,
distill to my veins their magic *jen shen,*
and raise from cold lips this spring song.

Every joining begets its severance,
a death to which we are entitled
as to life. Being what it is
a temporary absence, in our minds
you and I are free to triumph,
to perpetuate this woods, this walk, this day.

Paul Bennett

Husband and Wife

The sky is only three feet three away:
Bend your head if you go by foot,
Dismount if you go by horse.
— Chinese Folksong

Driving Ohio's meandering Route 78
west of Ringgold, he and she park
and walk to the rim of the world. Below,
in sun-drenched autumn air, hills
lie like great whales, like lovers,
in silence as deep as mid-ocean calm.

Fifty years into marriage, he and she
bend their heads to the gifts of October:
two sons, this chicory sky, these heaped hills
with their circles of trees, leaves
like gems from the Orient. Slowly taking in
this world, they speak their wonder, grow silent.

Appalachian Mettle

The Conference on War and Peace

I

Outside this conference hall I see
the marginal maple—ablaze in fall fire—
feeding on sun, rain, its slight bite of soil,
and I think of growing food,
the luxury of feeding oneself and neighbors,
the freedom of saying to a stranger:
"Come to my house, sit down at my table,
share what I have grown. Brother, sister."
Within walking distance of this hall
rain as light as dew settles upon the acre of earth
I have tended for some forty years, soil more fertile
today than the day I first turned it, spadeful
by spadeful. To love one bit of soil
is to know the earth. And to know the earth
in southern inclination—thirty degrees equals
three hundred miles nearer the sun
and its embrace: food, food, food, its way to
peace—is to chart the sun for Trinity.

II

Years ago an old gardener in our town
called on my father to borrow a boy
to help plant his musk-and-watermelon crop.
Youngest of six sons I got the assignment
of tedious labor, more tedious argument,
for as Father said: "With that good man
day begins at first light and runs till moon-up,

Paul Bennett

and listening to him you never know
whether he's discussing wife, garden, or life."
I spent summer's longest week
lost in the labyrinth of his words
and instead of pay at week's end
I got his promise: "We'll share the crop."
All summer long I took flak from my brothers
for being the biggest fool in town;
late that fall I came home from school
to find a wagonload of melons in our drive,
beside the load the grocer to buy them,
and later still, two loads more.

III

Many summer afternoons I drift away
from whatever work is at hand
to visit my white-peach-loving friend
who in the South Pacific took bamboo slivers
through his thick leather combat boots. I am
with him for countless operations—
big toe right foot, right leg at ankle,
left leg at knee, right leg at thigh.
Many summer afternoons I visit him
and see him as he was that last time—
hoisting himself by the harness
above his bed, his face aglow with drugs
and fever, but his voice steady, sure:
"Well old buddy, they're whittling me down
to give me a better stance on your hillside farm."
His face, his smile, his peace.

Appalachian Mettle

IV

Fine featured as carved ivory,
breathing like a frightened dove,
Yukiko Hoshino seats herself before me.
"In your country—how you say—one term
to learn American poetry—okay?"
I leave my desk to sit by her side
and we talk of American poetry.
As she stands to go, she says, "Thank you.
Dickinson and Whitman I know more, okay?"
Days become weeks; she says: "You are someone
to talk to American—okay?" She attends each class,
borrows my poetry anthology, and brings it
to our conferences wrapped in a handmade cover.
The book, I observe, opens automatically
to the poetry she wishes to discuss.
In deep winter snow our afternoons flower
in poetry of East and West. By early spring
she learns I took part in World War II. She smiles
and says, "They told me you were Navy—okay?
My father was Imperial Navy too—
how you say—your enemy?"
"Yes." With outstretched hand I say, "Crazy."
"Yes. You would kill him—he would kill you.
Crazy like crazy—okay?"

Paul Bennett

Counting the Mourning Doves

I have seen dreams die as hours creep to days,
days to seasons, to years that fly
like silk of milkweed in winter's wind.

Mauve mourning doves gather in Miami,
in this locale a blue spruce
that shelters from north wind one Viburnum
Carlesi, one sun-trapping bank of periwinkle.

In my heart I know it is not the presence
of quality in nature but its presence
in quantity that banks the fires of love.

Appalachian Mettle

Light Thoughts

I

I ponder much of late,
wake before dawn
amid hospitable dead friends
to anticipate
the reining in of stars,
homecoming of night hunters,
birds ordering the day,
the shipping out of clouds and rain,
the bundling up of rainbows
in a single drop of dew.

II

In the fertile hillside garden
I midwife seeds
with receiving blankets
of pulverized leaf and loam
till tubes form, warm,
initiate the capillary flow,
blood of being,
the sea, the sun,
the moon epitomized.
Fine as river silt
pinched between fingers
each pulse spells change,
torches night to flowers,
fruits and vegetables.

Paul Bennett

III

Unsettled as drifting mist,
quiet as sound caged
in the brown thrasher's throat
I move toward what will be.

IV

Late for the appointment
I take the elevator,
muse at its click-count of floors,
its label "Plunger-lift,"
ironic play of opposites,
complementary co-signs:
sun-moon, earth-sea.
Doors open slowly
and I am staring dumb
in time and space. My ears
perceive brown thrasher notes
echoing one word
in veins and distant woods:
how light love's substance is.

Appalachian Mettle

In the Shadow of the Pine

This ancient Scotch pine lived its faith;
worshiping sun, air, water, earth,
it made of me a fundamentalist.

Now, ax in hand, matches in pocket
I honor our forty years of friendship
by presiding at its crematory rites.

Unlike animals and birds, trees die
in public, their bodies racked with pain:
how far from fleshy green this brown skeleton.

With heavy heart and cleaving shoulder strokes
I lay my old friend low. As it goes down
it grabs my feet. I do not foresee my fall.

Luckily I land on shoulders and neck,
and roll with the blow. Numb as a stick
I lie still, waiting for my head to clear.

My first thought startles, then comforts me:
how much friendlier the earth has become
than when I fell to it in childhood games.

Paul Bennett

Fishing Again the Evolutionary Stream

Born with quick hands and feet,
never, never did I expect
to land this dead-fish right arm.

But we are what we become
and so this afternoon I sit
beside the threshing water

seeking to draw to my line
an opposable thumb,
a differentiated brain.

Appalachian Mettle

Wall Street Visit

I

From La Guardia the cabbie knew the route
to Wall Street, delivered me promptly
to the corporate building on whose 25th floor
Marvin Maple, the law firm's senior partner,
an old friend since 1947, held forth.
Linda, the secretary, ushered me to Marv;
he stood smiling, extending a square hand
that drew its enduring strength
from his youth in West Virginia's coalfields.

Laying an arm on my shoulder, he guided me
to his conference room, and told me
to make myself at home, he'd be a few minutes.
"I'm just finishing the most important brief
I've ever written, a class-action suit
before the Supreme Court. Ideas and logic
in a dance of words." He smiled.
"Would you care to guess the money involved?"

I met his eyes. "From your description, Marv,
I'd surmise you're talking millions."

His smile broadened, became a chuckle.
"To tell the truth, it's several billions."

"Thank God for the red hot pennies of our youth."

He clapped the law brief and walked away.

Paul Bennett

II

Standing at the conference room window I looked down
on a cameo; ship passing the Statue of Liberty.
In that instant I stood at conn of our old LST
in World War II, passing the Statue, in and out,
twice, once at night. As navigator
how damned glad I was the pilot boat had met our ship;
we steamed along under competent commands
of a grizzled harbor pilot who knew the whims
of East River, Hudson, and Atlantic currents
that mixed and flowed more treacherous
than any sea I'd sailed upon. The outbound ship
passed the Statue, and I thought of Marv
as a Rhodes scholar,
how that landmark would have looked
to him, fresh from rural West Virginia
headed off to England, and how inviting the Statue
two years later on his return from England,
Oxford scholarship, genteel ways, and grace
undergirding his West Virginia Law School learning.

III

The hush of the New York Club—private table,
linen damask, gleaming silver, heavy crystal—food
measured by taste and flavor not quantity,
gave way to West Virginia and Ohio coalfields:
that grave damp of an always-even-temperatured room
in a mine, where never for a moment could one forget
how far below ground one was, how ready one had to be
to ride, walk, crawl to daylight,

to feel the dread of night done and gone, fresh air
like cold cash in one's fist, the sun on one's face.
Remembering our past, Marv and I talked
of mines and miners and mine owners,
the need for John L. Lewis,
the record of the Sunday Creek Coal Company,
the land deeds that still enslave Kentucky
to those who pocket the blood money, salad oil
from the bodies that mine our coal, light our lights.

Marv recalled his father's telling of one fast coal loader
who came to grief at the hands of dynamite-laden friends
because he would not keep his hands off the coal columns
left to support the overhead. "Easy picking
for that damned loader, another lifeless human body."

I spoke of a fellow I knew in Ohio
who made a good living selling locust mine props,
but who had found it easy to increase his take
by passing poplar and pine as locust posts
to the ignorant son of a mine owner.

IV

How to relate means of living to destination?
This question—in Oxford English parlance, possessed
of merit—flickered to flame in lamp-light
on an Ohio farm, a West Virginia homestead,
years ago when Marv and I lived through time
without stop, among parents, aunts, uncles,
grandparents, in family-built houses, among generations,
who thrived in kind shadows of lamp-light,

Paul Bennett

apple-pungent fireplace warmth on face and outheld
hands, freezing cold drafts on our backs and butts.

Our chief means of living was words, words
our chief means of travel. Words that rolled
off male tongues—
hummed over, corrected and confirmed
by female voices—
words that bore promise of what had been,
was, would come,
once Laurel Creek gave up its winter flood
madness, and the roads and mines reopened.

Appalachian Mettle

Caretaker's Counsel

The man I sought stood among the stones:
he said he had plenty of time to talk markers,
meaning granite, not marble, and northern granite,
not southern. Your southern granite sops water,
see the shadows in those grays and reds,
that's decay and dissolution underway.
Water in stone is fatal, to use a word
you hear regular as clockwork hereabouts.
Or has been in every case I've studied
winter and summer for more than forty years.

Best buy for your money—I don't care the seller—
is solid granite from Vermont or New Hampshire
or the Pennsylvania mountains or Minnesota,
maybe as far west as North Dakota. Weight and freight
determine cost, as you'll discover;
for that reason, if no other, I wouldn't go in
for anything from India or Africa or South America,
for you just can't be sure. Dying is world-wide
universal; that's enough risking the unknown,
if you know what I mean.

You'll want your stone polished smooth, front and back
and top at least, to shed snow and rain
and stand up to weather. You can't be too careful
since it's likely to be the last thing you'll buy
with what I'd call coin of the realm. As to colors,
there's good blacks, grays, reds, and rainbows—
which is black and yellow and pink combined—
and you'd do well to suit your liking there.

Paul Bennett

For Dominick Consolo on His Seventy-Fifth

Whether by nature or nurture family is fate
and how fortunate our sovereign comforter
whose mother lived a long and generous life
humming a soft Sicilian tune,
whose shoemaker father sang along
below the cutting floor, a catcher of soles.

By genes our comforter took up trumpet
and travel, journeyed with Chaucer to Canterbury,
sailed with Melville the seven seas
observed from Arrowhead in the Berkshires,
fished the big two-hearted river, and as teacher
in Granville, Ohio, took up trolling,
catching Turner and Blaise, Boyer and Eisner,
all of them found to be keepers.

Appalachian Mettle

A Son Speaks of the Sun

Swear by thyself that at my death thy Sun
shall shine as it shines now.
— John Donne

Our fathers had a word for it: sun,
the star with invisible but invincible power
to light and heat and liven, make day as day,
and night as night. Consummate lover,
mother, father, its immense passion amazes:
with less than one two-billionths of its hot breath
it gives life to earth and lets us breathe.

Sun-begotten impulse leads me to tell the sun
of this son's love: I would name names,
set down glowing words like beams of light.
Sun alone knows where and how I began to write:
I say with David Snyder, young soldier
who died in WW I and I never met, but whose mother
welcomed me to David's library
when neither Ohio town or school had one.

My college roommate Charles Potter, from Long Island,
smiled like the sun when he said he always wanted
to come out west to go to school. The one for whom
our first son was named, he died February 18, 1942
when the destroyer TRUXTUN ran aground off Newfoundland
during the night in a violent storm at sea.
Death in sun's absence and only son's loss
left his widowed mother with no son save me.

Paul Bennett

The June morning I called on Jeanne Leonhart
at her Marietta home she stood tall and smiling
in a flowerbed of sun-kissed pink selene,
gold coreopsis, and blue and white delphiniums.
We married December 31, 1941
to start the war year right.
Riding night train after night train,
carrying sun's warmth
and promise of sons to come, she came
to whatever Atlantic port our LST had wallowed to.

War over, lovely Jeanne, generative as the sun itself,
designed a sun-worshipping house,
which she and I built
with our own hands in two summers' sweat;
she planted gardens of flowers the sun fell for,
and from her sun-blessed womb
she thrust two sons aloft.
Today her ashes warm the bank of a river we loved,
lilac blooms to their east, euonymus glows to their west;
apart, yet as one, she and I follow the sun
as it speeds on its way to eternity.

Appalachian Mettle

Family Reunion

Time after time I attend that family reunion
where beautiful long-legged cousins ran,
where shadows spilled from Mount Carmel Church
all the way to the lush meadows of Laurel Creek:

In after-dinner dusk Grandpa paces the long porch,
fiddle in hand, entertaining our parents
while we try our deer legs, chasing and catching
fireflies, locking them in jelly jar lanterns.

Grandpa tells of *the fire*, the farmhouse ablaze at 2 a.m.,
flames devouring seasoned oak, lath and plaster;
handhewn stone fireplace and chimney mouthed at,
gnawed on, spat out, still standing at dawn,
an island in a river of ruin. "I make the case,"
Grandpa says, "for peerless balance of right and wrong,
yin and yang, in the blood of this damned family."

I creep close to the porch to listen. A hand
steals my baseball cap off my head. Thinking "yes-yes,"
I duck away and shout: "No! No!" Soft hands grab me
from behind, cram my mouth with their perfume;
sleek curved bodies bear me to the ground, raise me,
drag me, captive into the shadows of the porch.

Grandpa is telling how Grandma and he took the train
to Maryland, there to seek resources for rebuilding,
reconcilement with Grandma's folks, who had been
I-told-you-so from the day she married him.
"In one long month," Grandpa says,

Paul Bennett

"we garnered not one red cent,
but back on this farm our four teenaged sons,
using borrowed tools,
built a house while we were gone,
a better house than the one we lost to fire,
a house mortgaged only to a sawyer friend."

Grandpa pauses to make eye contact with his sons;
I try to escape by crawling between Elsie's legs
but she closes them, folds her warm body over mine.
From that vantage point I hear Grandpa say: "You guys
have our eternal gratitude, but no special thanks.
After all, who seeded carpentry into this noble family?"

Narrative Poems

I am entrusted with many stories,
and have my own to tell.

— Kathleen Norris

Paul Bennett

The Saga of Sam Whitfield

Born in the Midwest in a wintry blast,
exposed to the common round—
family, school, church, state—
Sam Whitfield breathed spring winds fragrant
with pink, white, yellow,
fall winds fruited with apple pungency.
And he had reason to believe
courage and cowardice are step-brothers
that share one mother, experience;
courage fathered by familiarity,
cowardice by distance, the unknown;
and he had reason to ask:
"What of luck and no-luck?"

I. Indian River

The willow, large as an airy house,
languid as a braceleted arm trailing
from a red canoe in Indian River
overhung the green of the deep pool
where men and boys swam naked by day,
the entire town in suits by night.
There, slender and supple as eels
Sam Whitfield and Dan Painter learned
to swim, working their way upstream
from the wade-in gravel bank
till they could drop
from the long-roped water maple.
Diving came easy when, like minks,
they ran the riverbank by day,
cleaved by night the silver water.

Appalachian Mettle

Claiming the village swimming hole
by squatters' rights, they could but stare
when they visited Ned and Ted Rink's
luxurious country home
and were led to a dammed five-foot brook
forming a pool eighteen inches deep,
twenty-five or thirty feet across.
King without lieges or castle,
Whitfield thought, for Ted Rink,
taller, heavier, older by two years,
ruled the schoolground with fists of stone.

"You don't swim here?" Dan Painter said.
"Oh sure we do," Ned Rink replied.
"Ted's better than me. He'll show you how."
And Ted did, slipping out of his clothes,
wading in, stooping, stretching out,
kicking up mud, and crawling on his hands
amid darting minnows and water skippers.
"You swim like a fish," Dan said,
avoiding the sheen of flung water and eyeing
Whitfield, who nodded.
"I'll bet you two could swim Indian River."
"Maybe I couldn't," Ned spoke as one
who had learned humility the hard way,
"but Ted could—"
                              "Could and will!"
Ted called. "Next time we come to town."

There, under sun-filtering willow and maple,
four naked boys stared across flowing green.
"It's pretty wide," Ned observed. "Yeah,
Whit and me'll drop in," Dan said, "and show

how deep it is." He grabbed the rope,
swung, and jack-knifed above the river;
he came up, flipped his head, and said:
"I'll let down right here, Ted,
and show you how deep it really is."
His fingertips lingered, waved, and disappeared.
Ned bit his lower lip and glanced
at his brother. "It ain't that deep!"
"It is," Whitfield said. "Eight feet
or so right off the bank, twelve or more toward the
middle."
                         Fear fought pride
in Ted's eyes. Terror closed
on Whitfield's throat; he sought
to shape words to inform a king
he didn't know what he didn't know:
in a strange land he wore no clothes.
"You coming in?" Dan asked, lolling back.
"Hell yes, I am." Ted leaped
as he had in his sunny wading pool.
For years Whitfield would measure nightmares
by that face registering the feel
of nothingness: nothing to touch, nothing
but water, rushing
to fill a mouth opened to shout
the word the water rushed to silence.

Whitfield dived and swam deep,
fought free of clenching arms and legs,
cupped hands to the gargoyle face. Buffeted
and beat, with Dan's help, he bore aloft
the threshing burden: a king berserk.
Against the bank they pinned the body,

Appalachian Mettle

fixed clawing hands on willow fingers,
then boosted the babbling boy ashore,
where he lay head-down on sloping bank,
water frothing from mouth and lungs.

II. The Crossing

When driving the basketball team to games,
Bert Dryer, coal hauler by day,
wore his military jacket and cap. Festooned
and trailing streamers of scarlet and grey crepe,
Bus 5, notorious for fumes
and a faulty heater, loaded in fog:
the two coaches, first and second team players
(Whitfield among them, least of the twenty),
the roly-poly red-haired insurance agent
schoolboard member score-keeper,
and the two team managers, who, as usual,
wallowed on board last (except for
the ladies and privileged Mr. K.).

"Gentlemen, the ladies," announced Mr. K.,
ushering on board three cheerleaders,
raincoats hiding gazelle legs, and Whitfield's
history teacher in her red velveteen suit
(she his favorite, he hers,
whose smile mouthed at his heart's core).

Last to board: Randolph A. Kleer,
the monumental manual arts instructor,
scout master, cock of the school,
of top-sergeant mien, commanding voice,
who rode point man at the door

maintaining order going and coming.
"Gentlemen," he had growled in the locker room,
"there'll be no feeling up of our female guests
including Miss Peters—not one pass or pinch—
so long as I'm in charge. And Whitfield,
keep your huge animal where it belongs,
padlocked within the barn, preferably asleep.
What you blushing about, boy? You're burning red."

"Loaded out, Bert," Mr. K. announced;
"all hands on board, so let her rip."
Bert Dryer worked the lever closing the door,
and snapped off the inside lights.
"We'll slipper through this soup," he said,
deftly shifting gears of the purring bus,
stabbing the fog with brights,
then quickly dimming to cast
a fifty-foot bowl of white ahead.
"Right," Mr. K. exclaimed, "right as ritual!
We'll creep through fog and surprise the Rexville
squad like Washington crossing the Delaware."

Mr. K's. hand settled on Miss Peters' knee,
his voice rose: "Merrily we roll along,
roll along, roll along, o'er the deep blue sea."
Miss Peters excused herself and moved to sit
next to Whitfield, behind Bert Dryer,
to help decipher the white center line
as Bus 5 crept out of town.
In the low fog bed between canal and river
Bert Dryer down-shifted and felt his way toward the
double-tracked railroad crossing.
Miss Peters whispered at Whitfield's ear:

"The signal lights are flashing."
"Right as ritual," exclaimed Mr. K.,
"one if by land, two if by sea."
Bert Dryer braked to a stop, and worked
the door. "I can almost see—"
"My hand before my face," asserted Mr. K.;
he climbed down and stood beside the bus.
"I hear it now!" there was a moment's hush,
a whistle, then the clamor of wheels
on the farthest track. "Now we know
exactly where we are and why," announced Mr. K.
"When it goes, we go." He got in.

The freight passed, caboose lights barely visible.
Bert Dryer opened the door and waited.
"Silence!" Mr. K. commanded. "Silence in the
bus!" The signal lights were flashing: *red, red, red.*
"They've been known to stick—malfunction—
in this kind of weather," Mr. K. proclaimed
as he got out, knelt, and laid his ear
to the track. "Metal carries sound,
hence the invention of the telephone."
He listened again, then arose and beckoned.

Bert Dryer glanced at the red signal,
live red. "I'd rather not, we'll wait."
"Bert," Mr. K. commanded, "come along!
I've tested the track, the signal's stuck."
Bert Dryer hesitated, edged forward,
the front wheels cleared the track,
Mr. K. swung on board. "This kind of night
brings out the scout—"
Bert Dryer jammed gas pedal to floor,

the bus leaped to escape the eye,
the on-rushing maw that gobbled fog,
tore and devoured the trailing crepe;
he let out a breath, a sigh,
and drove on, letting Bus 5 settle back
to the patient speed the fog allowed.
Whitfield who had out-stared the on-coming eye
with a wish for the woman beside him,
heard a voice murmur at his ear:
"As sure as hell was meant for fools
Bert Dryer will drive in heaven."

III. Landing Ship, Tank

The day before, they had done the locks
from Cristobal to Gulf of Panama,
headed west. In the blue Pacific gulf
Whitfield had adjusted to change of sea—
feet, legs, stomach, heart and head—
long slow sweep after Atlantic chop
his hammock's drift like the cushioned swing
of his mother's womb.
                    All afternoon
he had tended Al Barker, Machinist's Mate First,
in welding the starboard smallboat davit,
affixing it again to the deck,
and between blinks of blue arcs
had beheld in peripheral sight
countless warblers flitting,
gold sparks gathered from jungle trees
when the LST rode the lock, now
chilled by fresh Pacific breeze,
searching for sun in Navy gray steel.

Appalachian Mettle

At evening chow Whitfield and Barker
joshed Machinist's Mate Cannon—
shoddy outfielder, perfect fart snatcher—
who had sat on the stepladder
in the compartment below, catching
stray sparks in a water-filled fire bucket.
"Dog-do trumps cat shit," Cannon said,
"you buzzards don't think I rode that ladder
all that time. You worked so slow
I set the damned pisspot on the ladder
and caught a smoke and snooze on deck."
"Asshole," Barker growled, "suppose
we had shifted welds while you goofed off?"

Whitfield came off his twenty hundred bow watch
and sank into his hammock's pouch.
Minutes—or hours—later,
fire quarters sounded:
fire in the hold below the weld.
Out of hammock, legs into dungarees,
sockless feet in shoes, bare of chest,
watch cap on head, Whitfield fled,
he and his fire-eating detail
to where the hatch belched black and
deck plates simmered, rusty red,
where Captain Barr, having learned
the fire was next to the ammunition locker,
placed Ensign Wand in charge
and found it necessary to take the conn
to steer the ship through miles of calm.

Paul Bennett

"Running won't save his ass if the ammo blows,"
Barker snarled. "Give Whitfield and me
the fucking fire hose, rope our waists
and lower away." And it was done.
Whitfield drew a breath free of smoke, then
into the hot-laddered smoke hole
two half-naked apes on two slim lines
wrestling the writhing water hose,
praying two lines would hold, one breath
would last the descent to hell.
Seconds as hours, seconds as lives,
sizzle and pop, a heady aerial feel,
water played on smoking grids,
compartment awash in boiling ship's stores,
breath spent, played out like the life
it was, slowly spent, the dead-fish yank
drawing him back to the land of air.

Lying in spotlight on deck, he and Barker
coughed and coughed, cried and coughed
till Barker caught a breath
in his blackface comic's mouth: "Whitfield,
you'll live to fry in hell." His eyes' whites
rolled as a warbler dipped above his head.

Officer of the Deck Wand duly recorded
in the ship's log: *Two hundred three: Watch
discovered a small fire in forward hold,
all hands manned fire stations. Captain Barr
took command at scene. Fire tapped out
at three hundred thirteen. Negligible damage
to vessel, no injury to officers or crew.*

Appalachian Mettle

IV. The Flight

In the western reach of cerulean sky
Whitfield saw one fast-moving storm cloud
like a fat gray goose in flight,
as though the ancient twin-engined plane
had already taken off. Dead ahead
two attendants, smiling, checked tickets
and welcomed the milling crowd on board.
Last to enter, Whitfield thought:
These old sky boats are like a school bus,
always room for one more.

Seating himself by the right window
as if assigned to tend that motor,
he heard the doors clang shut,
engines start, rev to rhythm,
attendants' voices, seat belts' click,
then felt the turning, taxiing,
lunging aloft, and saw, underneath,
flowing concrete, brown corn rows
falling away to fields,
persons to ants, cars to toys,
and close at hand the gauze of clouds.

Undoing his seat belt, Whitfield
glanced to his engine—stared transfixed
at snake-tongued flame, puff
of smoke, white then black.
He motioned the attendant and pointed;
she raised a finger to her lips, moved
to the cockpit door. The co-pilot
leaped forth, beheld, exclaimed:

Paul Bennett

"Oh, my god—my god, no!" His face,
wrenched in disbelief,
hung in the doorway long
after he had gone inside.
Out the window, now speckled
with oil, Whitfield saw the propeller
stop, then idly circle.
Over the intercom the pilot said:
"Fasten all seat belts, we're returning—"

Whitfield heard the single engine left
straining, responding, taking the load,
throbbing like a runaway heart.
The fat man opposite grabbed
two pillows from overhead,
hid his face; a second man began
to curse the airline, shouted "Goddamn,"
collapsed. Somewhere a child
began to cry; his mother's voice
rose, saying: "Jeffey, Jeffey,
we'll be all right; we'll be all right."
In a long slow turn the plane
was sinking, creeping closer
to its good motor. Whitfield felt
the downward glide, saw a cornfield rising:
rows, stalks, leaves, tassels in their
feathery blowing, then concrete
down which sped three red trucks.

Appalachian Mettle

Building a House

I never in all my walks came across a man
engaged in so simple and natural an occupation as
building his house.
— Henry Thoreau

I

By night rats gnawed our apartment walls,
by day Jeanne and I scoured town and countryside
in search of housing or building site, but found none.
One October afternoon, biking the long ridge road
on which the college stood, we came on a briary hillside
tilted south, overlooking a gold beech woods.
"Why buy a hillside?" the owner-farmer said,
"all you'd be getting is sunshine and fresh air."
"What more comes with a building site?" I asked.
"Soil that grows blackberries will grow vegetables
and—with luck—fruit trees and family."
Jeanne said: "I love the land, the view."

All fall we fought off rats, read and pondered
housing: how and what to build.
We drew up plans distilled from dreams
begun on campus as a flippant courtship vow:
someday we'll build a signboard shack;
dreams of a decade—four years at Ohio University;
three war years of New York, Boston, Norfolk,
San Diego, the Atlantic and Pacific;
two years of Harvard, Cambridge, the River Charles;
one year-long Maine winter—our hopes

Paul Bennett

embraced Frank Lloyd Wright,
wedded Walden to Monticello,
but how does one build on fresh air and sun?

II

Fall passed, winter found us long on waste paper,
short on cash, for we must do on instructor's pay—
what was left after apartment rent (rats came free),
feeding and clothing Jeanne, infant son Charles, and me.
Last of our Navy nest egg had gone for the land,
to purchase fruit trees, drill a water well,
to put up an aluminum shed from which
to build the house,
to buy rough-sawed wild cherry lumber
to be kiln dried, milled and dressed as panelling.

All winter we planned and talked around,
consulting a retired carpenter, who advised us
to run 1x10-inch redwood siding vertically,
paralleling interior paneling, and to use 2x4s
every two feet between the studs to nail into.
I biked miles to a sawmill to buy the cherry lumber;
we both biked to the hardware and library; we biked
and talked, for travel and talk are cheap
when legs and lungs are strong. We listed our needs:
three bedrooms, kitchen, living room, bath—
(remembering home), a bath and a half—
a one-car garage.
We planned a house to own, to grow into;
plainly we wanted more than we could pay for.

Appalachian Mettle

III

Our materials list grew and grew;
we calculated costs and saw room sizes shrink
and shrink. One night when Jeanne had gone to bed
and I was fathoms deep in impossibility
I suddenly saw a way: if we put bedrooms and bath
in the basement and built the house into the hill—
if we terraced east and west—*Viola*: We could have
underground bedrooms with full-sized windows
and gain space like found gold. All the next day
we redrafted plans and watched the tiny living room
grow to a generous 16½ x 32 feet.

Ideas came fast: if we used an open-beamed ceiling
with open stairwell (finished off as art gallery),
and on the opposite wall, facing south,
five plate-glass windows
set out at an angle to catch the sun, we'd enlarge
the room, gain solar heat, and have space for bookcases
under the windows; the window seats themselves
could be filled in early spring with plastic trays
to hold seeds of tomatoes, peppers, shastas, delphiniums—
all the seedling vegetables and flowers we wished—
if we did all that, we could live in a veritable greenhouse,
have solar heat, ground-insulated bedrooms and bath,
entertain the sun as royal guest all winter long—
Jeanne and I talked softly throughout the night
as we sought to love a house into being.

Paul Bennett

IV

Next day I biked to the building site
and using the aluminum shed as model, marked out
the low-arching winter sun, how to situate the house.
While I calculated shed-roof overhang and shutters
for summer shade, Jeanne,
with professional chartist's touch,
finished out the floor plans to scale, and made
watercolor perspectives of the house-to-be.

That weekend, with detailed materials list costed out
to the dollar, and plans and perspectives
tucked in my bike basket, I pedaled off
to make the rounds of banks and lending institutions.
(What an education in economics that!)
One by one I made my visit and crossed a new name
off the list. Not one loan officer would listen
to my full explanation or cast more than a glance
at the list of materials, Jeanne's artful drawings.
Wait—there was one, a savings-and-loan president
who said the watercolor perspectives caught his eye—
would I please leave the plans with him till Tuesday?
Would I? I all but kissed the man good-bye.

V

Should I get to live in heaven
never will I forget that Tuesday morning bike ride—
six sunny miles seemed a hundred yards downhill.
In that lending institution I was ushered
to an inner sanctum carpeted in dark-green pile,

123

just past the sacred vault itself. There I beheld a ritual:
the banker reached behind him for our plans,
snapped off the rubber band and flipped it up his wrist,
shook out the list of materials, laid out the plans,
leaned back, fixed his eyes on me, and said:
"Young man, who told you you could build a house?"
His tone partially revealed a butcher knife,
and taken unawares, I murmured, "No one—
what I mean is, people don't come to you and say..."
"Well, let me do you a favor, a big favor.
I'll tell you straight out: you can't do it!
And as for this—" his fleshy palm flattened the plans—
"I'd be an ass to lend money entrusted to this institution
on such an idiotic undertaking. Look at this:
bedrooms in the basement! And this!"
He jabbed a forefinger with digging nail
against the materials list: "A drilled well—
one hundred and fifty-seven feet deep—at that figure!
You'd never get a well drilled at that rate!"

"Sir, sir," I protested, but he was a pit bull
whose jaws were at my throat.
"And look at this living room—
what are those dimensions?
—sixteen by thirty-two feet,
that to be panelled in three-quarter inch wild cherry—
at that rate per board foot? Never, never!"
"Sir," I said, "if you notice, all those items
marked by asterisk: the aluminum shed, the well,
the cherry panelling—those items marked are done;
the well is drilled and paid for; the cherry wood
is in the shed curing, and I have a mill's commitment

to tongue and groove it at that price.
The explanations show what is done, what's to do."
"Nevermind!"
He crammed materials' list into plans, rolled them,
snapped the rubberband in place, and launched the roll
across his desk. I caught it as it fell,
and felt my blood rise. But before I spoke I recalled
a day I had served as aide to a land-locked admiral
and been exposed to a command performance. I said:
"Well, thank you for your time, your advice."

Something in my tone seemed to touch him,
for as I moved toward the door, his voice changed:
"Just a moment, just a moment, young man..."
He came around his desk, holding out his hand.
"I'm trying to panel my den—the den of my home,
you understand—in wild cherry wood, and I'd—
well, if you could tell me where you found that cherry—
where did you buy it, may I ask?"
"Sir," I said, ignoring his hand to meet his eye,
"I found it over the hills south of town."
I turned and left, unlocked my bike before the bank,
and pedaled slowly the long road home.

VI

I told our troubles to a friend who said: "Buck up!
Economics is not to be understood but practiced,
and when it is, money flows like ground water."
He volunteered to co-sign a personal note;
the local banker, who had cast a cold eye on our plans,
now smiled, and deposited cash to our checking account.

Appalachian Mettle

The day spring vacation began I bought a pick,
a shovel, and contractor's wheelbarrow, and started
to excavate the basement. For ten days (including April 1)
I dug and hauled earth from dawn till dark; I dug
like a groundhog, stopping only to eat and sleep.
I moved what seemed a Joycean mountain
and had a sizeable hole when my brother-in-law came by;
he surveyed the piled earth and hole, then kindly asked:
"Have you ever heard of a machine called a bulldozer?"

Next morning I phoned a dozer man named Jack Frost,
and on April 9 he arrived on site. He moved more earth
in fifteen minutes than I had moved in ten days. He stopped,
climbed down from his idling machine, and said:
"My job is easy; someone had cut sod, saved topsoil."
I thumbed my chest. "Meet the fool."
He nodded as if he had already guessed, then mounting
his purring calico cat, completed the excavation—
total time on job: forty-five minutes. I learned from that
and had a truck deliver ready-mixed concrete
for the footing trench on which to lay foundation blocks.

Weekends till school was out and I could work full time.
Jeanne and I laid up concrete blocks. On June 6
my brother-in-law, man of all trades, joined me
on the job, and concrete blocks rose, row on orderly row
(one builds toward the heavens, after all) and we laid
an extra row to give height for finishing basement rooms,
and then the solid cap, the anti-termite blocks.
Skyrockets from the town's July 4 celebration two miles off
announced our house plate bolted into place, floor joists
and subflooring laid. Sitting at what

Paul Bennett

would be living room height
we found ourselves looking across to moonlit traceries
of fine beech leaves, contemplating what came next:
the upward surge of studs, the oak-beamed ceiling,
the insulated air space, the built-up roof.

VII

By August 1 the house was under roof and roughed in,
visible if not vital. Now we thought of heart, brain,
digestive tract: the furnace, electrical and water systems,
the long gut of the sanitary sewer. Our brother-in-law,
who could see intricate things done and do them,
counseled Jeanne and me: on furnace,
choose extra BTUs, it will heat for less and last;
on electric lines, plan extra circuits,
more outlets than needed;
the water system all copper, the best deep-well pump;
on septic lines, use fired-clay pipes, tanks the same—
they endure. We listened, and aided by his skilled
hands and good-humored guidance, built accordingly.

Two tasks only proved to be beyond our powers:
the bending of sheet metal for the furnace plenum
(we installed standard pipes where we could),
and the setting-in of the five plate-glass windows.
We hired these jobs done, and were glad we did,
for as the glaziers were installing the plate windows,
a carelessly driven nail caught one corner
and sent out a crack like a spider's web.
"Aw, what the hell," exclaimed the workman,
"we'll cut that one down a bit and sell it
on another job."

Appalachian Mettle

Now as time called the tune,
and we worked against vacation's end, school's beginning,
our muscles and nerves overtaxed, our tempers short,
we began to have many visitors, self-invited inspectors
who had heard of an upside-down house being built
that required their personal stamp of approval.
The local architectural expert drove past
one rainy evening, saw the shed roof and announced:
"The Bennetts are building a modernistic chicken coop."
The local banker, who rode the architect's cocktail circuit,
began to be fretful that the house, when done,
might not be appraised at a sufficient sum
to cover the money lent on the personal note—
before fall arrived, he grew cool, distant, official.

VIII

The first week in September school began,
our brother-in-law went back to his employment,
and each evening Jeanne and I ate early,
loaded Charlie in my bike basket ("Easy son, away we go"),
and set off to the building site. Night after night we worked:
mixing mortar and laying industrial flooring brick
in entry way, kitchen, bedrooms and bath;
laying oak flooring in living room; installing
oak panelling on all interior walls except living room—
three-quarters inch white oak tough as steel,
which had to be gnawed through with sharpest hand saw
(and smelled like cat when cut), which demanded
much hand fitting, causing me to master the hand rasp
as well as hand saw, wood so tough each nail hole
had to be pre-drilled. Such wood gave reason

Paul Bennett

to love Jeanne more with each board fitted
into place, for her patience and persistence shamed me.
Her smaller hands would clamp a recalcitrant board,
lock it against her hip vice-tight for rasping,
or work it into place upon the wall,
and hold it there with the wrecking bar
until I could fasten it to furring strip or stud.

By three or four a.m., a night's work done,
we'd awaken Charlie, set him, still half asleep,
in my bike basket ("Easy does it son,
we're headed back now, hold on tight"), and pedal off
to our college apartment. Many nights on the return
we had a great horned owl for escort, for he found
two cyclists with child utterly fascinating: he'd fly
from one fence post to another with the swish of great wings,
sit to eye us, and like lightning turn his puzzled head
as we sped by. Our nightly processions finally awakened.
the campus patrolman, who caught up with me and Charlie—
riding some distance ahead of Jeanne—beneath the shadow
of the girls' dormitory. Thrusting his searchlight in my eyes
he demanded: "Halt! Halt, I say!
Where did you get that child?"
His tone implied illicit happenings in the dormitory.
Pushing light aside, I said:
"He's our son, his mother will come—
comes riding even now. Mr. Watchman,
meet Mrs. Bennett."

Appalachian Mettle

IX

Thanksgiving Day, clear and bright for Ohio,
we moved to our new home. Much was done,
much to do, and Jeanne and I knew which
was which, and how to live with our errors.
We put up the 1x10-inch redwood Anzac siding,
nailing it exactly as our carpenter friend,
who had gone to his reward, had specified.
Eventually we hung the interior birch doors,
and panelled the living room in random-width cherry
treated with linseed oil and satin-finish varnish
—plain is rich. And we were delighted, for what we
had done we did with the help of relatives and friends.

We were tempted to invite a savings-and-loan president
to inspect the house, but we settled for three
FHA architects: one from Cincinnati, two from
Columbus. They inspected and pried into each detail,
then appraised the house at three times the value
required to cover the personal loan,
restoring Jeanne and me to the local banker's graces.
Later, the architect from Cincinnati
brought one of his clients a hundred miles
to see what could be done with sunshine and fresh air.
And the architect who taught at Ohio State University
came with his camera and took pictures for slides, saying,
"This will be the only house in my graduate course
not designed and built by professionals."
I said to Jeanne for her small ears only:
"Designed by trial and error, built by rasp and bicycle."

Paul Bennett

Homer Only: The Dowser

For more than forty years Jeanne and I have known
what takes place on our hillslope cannot be:
huge harvest of flowers, fruits, vegetables
nourished in woods' soil hauled in by wheelbarrow,
fed by a never-ending stream of sweet water
pumped from a well at precisely that spot to best serve
garden and house, a well one-hundred and fifty feet
deep, ever-flowing, never failing, when nearby wells,
two fifty and three hundred feet deep, run dry.
All this greenery and water-grown goodness ours
because on his deathbed Homer Only told us:
"Cultivate bluebirds, speak to 'em in their tongue
'Pretty birdy, pretty birdy,' to get back their song."

He arrived one sunny October afternoon
at our newly purchased hillside building lot
when Jeanne and I were sawing out 2x4 rafters
to build a shed, the shed to be used to store
materials from which to build our house.
He drove a battered red Ford pickup, sporting
unpainted cattle racks and wind-raveled half-inch
cattle ties; he wore a sweat-stained grey fedora,
a red-checked flannel shirt, deep-cuffed chino pants,
and eight-inch high work shoes—all showing
battle scars, signs of wear and weather.

He had come by, he said, to let us know
he was our down-the-road neighbor, one
who dealt in cattle 'n this 'n that,
and he could do drowsing for a deep water well,
if and when that was called for.

Appalachian Mettle

I motioned to Jeanne and stopped pulling the saw,
rested it on the sawhorse between us.
"We've had a colleague from Catalona College,
a professional geologist," I said, "show us
where to drill our water well." I pointed to
a waist-high stake at the lower end of our long lot.

"My name is Homer Only," our visitor said;
he fixed me with his bright right eye
while his cloudy left, given to wandering,
shifted from Jeanne's face to the distant white stake.

I laid down the hand saw and shook his hand,
introduced myself and Jeanne.

                              "Homer Olney?" Jeanne asked.
"Homer Only," he said, his good eye twinkling,
"but friends call me only *Homer*. And
don't let me stop your sawing." He seated himself
on a stack of cement blocks, reached out
and began to sift pine sawdust through his fingers,
raised a double handful to his nose and snifted.
"I own the beech woods beyond the stake," he said.

"You own that marvelous beech woods?" Jeanne said.
"All that good woods' soil waiting to grow flowers?"

"I do," Homer said. "Trees make soil." He lifted
one handful after another of sawdust, letting it fall
in golden shower, letting some of it dribble into
his open pant cuff. To Jeanne he said: "You look
like a lady who'd be good at raising flowers."
                              "Thanks," Jeanne said.

Paul Bennett

I sawed out the rafter Jeanne held locked between hip
and sawhorse; she lifted it to the finished stack,
then reached for another and held it to the pattern
for me to pencil in the sawing line. "You're right
on the mark," I said to Homer. "She's wild
to raise flowers, and I hope to raise
vegetables, fruits, berries, children."

"Being a neighbor you're welcome to all
the woods' soil you can haul in a wheelbarrow."
Homer's bright eye smiled on Jeanne: "The soil's yours
to use as long as you like if you'll agree
to put it back when you're done."
                    "Thank you," Jeanne said.
Blushing, she added: "We both expect to raise a family."

"You're in luck," Homer said to me, but tilted his head,
shifting both eyes to Jeanne as if to get a fix on her
child-bearing potential. After a moment he went on:
"If you mean to homestead garden—raise flowers,
vegetables, berries, fruit, family,
maybe even have a grape barber—
you'll probably want your water well more handy
than that white stake way off yonder."

"We thought we'd drill right there," I said:
"Henry Blauser is to be our well driller."

"I know Henry Bowser; he'll do right by you."

Jeanne explained: "That stake's where Percy Wick,
the college geologist, by studying his colored charts,
thought there'd be the best water-bearing sand."

Appalachian Mettle

"I can do a bit of water drowsing," Homer said,
"if and when it's called for."
                    "Dows..." I began,
but Jeanne cut me off: "We understand water wells
hereabouts run two fifty to three hundred feet deep."

"Expensive feet," I said.
                    "Drilling costs money!"
Homer added: "It's not like when first settlers came
'n looked for 'n found a year-round spring,
then built beside it." He paused in dribbling sawdust,
then bent his head and dribbled on.

Jeanne and I sawed out two rafters, and I nudged
the sawdust toward Homer's waiting hands.
He accepted the sawdust with his wobbly eye,
keeping his good eye fixed on Jeanne. Finally he said:
"My well is only one hundred 'n thirty feet deep,
with thirty feet of standing water in it."

"You mean it? Jeanne said.
                    "I said it." Homer smiled.
"How is the water?" I asked. "Hard or soft?"

"Soft, 'n sweet as maple, steady as a lake,
which means it ain't never run dry."
"Well," Jeanne said, smiling, and looked at me.

"I can do a bit of water drowsing," Homer said,
"if and when it's called for."
                    Lips rising,
I spoke to Jeanne: "Those words sound almost familiar.
Have we heard them before or do I imagine it?"

Paul Bennett

Jeanne laughed, then Homer laughed. "Homer," she said,
"do you use a special wood in your dowsing?"

"Generally," Homer said, "I like pussy willow
or crick willow, if it's handy." He waited.

"Jeanne said: "Willow goes with water!" I looked at her,
shook my head. "It's commonsense," she said.

"I've drowsed some with lilac 'n redbud," Homer said.
His bright eye was exploring our lot's scrub growth.

I stopped sawing, for Jeanne had let the rafter slip;
her eyes too were on the fringe-of-the-wood trees
bordering our long lot. "How about dogwood?" she asked.

"It might do," Homer said. "Probably would." He paused.
"I'd know oncst I got aholt of it."

"The wood itself would tell you?" I said. I hoped
Jeanne could hear the red flags she ignored.

Leaning forward, Homer began dumping sawdust
from his pant cuffs, restoring it to the pile
beneath the sawhorse. "I have a pocketknife."
He got to his feet and motioned toward a dogwood.

"Of course there'd be a fee for *drowsing*?" I said.

"Ordinary, yes," Homer said. "But for neighbors no."

"We mean to drill where the white stake..." I began.

"It wouldn't hurt to have Homer confirm it," Jeanne said.

"Regular geologists—Catalona College folks, I mean—
don't always do the same as I do," Homer said.
"That's part of what makes dogs run foxes."
He moved off to the dogwood tree, cut
a three-quarter inch branch, returned,
planted it butt down, and began removing,
one by one, the many crimson-green leaves.
As he worked, he talked: "Years ago Nell and me
went to hear the President of Catalona speak.
What he said made sense, but he didn't say it
the way I'd of said it if I'd been speaking."

"Was it Pat Korner?" I said. "He was a spell-binder."

"No, the one before him, Miles Rhenquist."

"Before our time," I murmured to Jeanne.

"He was a right good speaker," Homer said.
"You could tell he'd studied words, 'n knew
what they meant. It was what they called
a Backie Laurie address. He got going
'n talked for an hour and six minutes. Nell timed him."

"Probably meant it for an hour, just ran over
a bit—a good speaker will sometimes do that," I said.

Jeanne had stooped to help Homer pinch the last leaves
from the dogwood branch. She looked to him and asked:
"What did he say, "I'll bet *you* remember?"

Paul Bennett

Homer shifted his good eye from his leafing.
"He said two things: Save your pennies 'n plant
dogwoods." Homer stood up, flexed and bent the
dogwood branch, and began a steady pacing back
and forth, raising and lowering the fresh-stripped
branch. Satisfied with what he felt he paced to the
upper lot line where I had traced in lime
the unbuilt house.

Minutes later, midway down to the slope where
Jeanne and I had staked out our garden spot,
he stopped, turned, turned round again,
swinging the dogwood wand back and forth, back
and forth. Then he called out:
"Water close, well goes here!"

I looked at Jeanne, raised my hands, groaned;
she smiled and raised her shoulders in a who-knows
salute. I said: "I just don't believe in dowsing."
She said: "Homer calls it drowsing." Look closely,
he keeps his good eye closed sleep tight."

                    She was right.

Homer had kicked out a chunk of sod; now he turned
and went back to the top of the sloping lot
and rewalked the ground with the same result.
This time, using his pocketknife, he shaped a point
on the dogwood wand, sank it deep into the ground
and that is where—at Jeanne's insistence—
Henry Blauser drilled our *only Home*r well.

Appalachian Mettle

Kirk's Hospital Visit

I

Hospitals always undergo repairs:
where we once assumed permanency
all is flux, entry is by side door,
the elevator does not work,
we climb stairs that smell
of cabbage cooking.

There is no number on the door,
the man we seek is not present
in these eyes; it is his second stroke
and I wonder: could one week
make such difference, or glasses
or teeth? He is of the dead,
straining against restraining straps
that hold him to the bed.

His daughter pulls him to her,
lends her breast to cushion his head;
while he concentrates upon my name
I bring two chairs and seek escape
in other voices. The blind man next
is ninety years old; he utters it
with every breath. He has control
of nothing; a nurse and her aide come,
flip the curtain halfway round
and clean him, then begin to treat
the gangrenous toes of his right foot.

Paul Bennett

The nurse, who fills her uniform
like a sausage, murmurs to her gum-chewing aide:
"This is the way one goes,
rotting in the extremities."
The blind man, a retired grocer
whose worst crime was shorting weight,
mutters: "Why are you doing that to me?"

His words remind me of one I knew
who wanted only love, the act of love,
and had been betrayed in it.
Then I think of a great king
trading his known kingdom for one
infinite in time and space,
alone and lost upon a distant shore.

II

Man coagulates self, place, a point
of time, and I recall this man
as maker of harness whose needles, knives, awls
throughout these many years
since he shifted to automobiles
have rested neat as an ordered mind,
bright as the horizoned sun
within his hand-crafted box, awaiting
the call that soon must come
when he declares himself to worms
a fellow worker in new leather.

And I recall the gnarled English author
who said: "I gave up medicine

for fiction so I had to devote
the same energies and time to writing
I would have given to medicine;
everyday after breakfast I sat down
and wrote—everyday without fail
I sat down and wrote."
"What happened," the interviewer asked,
"when you had no ideas, nothing to write?"
"Then I wrote my name, just my name
until in boredom I had a thought
upon which I could write—besides,
it helped me know who I was and am."

III

The blind man in the next bed farts,
the nurse shakes her head and smiles,
the nurse's aide blushes and tugs the curtain,
the odor mingles with that of cabbage cooking.

IV

The daughter of the harness maker
tells him his Paul Scarlets thrive
in full bloom. He responds
with furred tongue: "That's good.
Remember how their fragrance
filled the yard in the morning sun?"
She smiles and nods to me. I think:
daughters spend their lives seeking
to mate their fathers, to recreate
that relationship they had at one remove

by birth. She would have preferred
instinctively to be one who said *yes*,
but denied by something indescribable,
she has become one who said *no*
and could not help herself do more.

The nurse's aide, cruising the cubicle,
finds a vagrant clothes hanger
and slaps it onto its quarter-inch rod;
in the closet the vigor of her action
reverberates loud, almost musical.

V

Bending again at the blind man's feet
the nurse's aide explains: "The best program ever,
all about how to defend yourself
against all-out rape. This neat guy said
in event you're convinced it's an all-out attack
there are only two ways to save yourself:
you can either blind your attacker
by pushing your thumbnails in his eyes
or you can seize a testicle and squash it—
either way you incapacitate your assailant."

The blind man moans: "Why are you
doing that to me?" I think:
she believed I could do anything—
almost anything—I set my hand to;
she came to me and told me so,
instinctively she said *yes*
when the other said *no*,

could a father have been the difference?

The nurse's aide says: "He will,
either way he will. He will let you
take his face in your hands, or his testicles,
that's just the natural thing
in the act of love, this neat guy said,
and then you can sink your thumbnails deep
into his eyes or grab a testicle and squeeze!"

VI

From the wall speaker the nurse's name.
She says to the aide: "We're all but done,
you can finish here." But the aide
is elsewhere and she announces:
"Let the punishment equal the crime."
The nurse, turning to go, pauses to say:
"That will hold you, Mr. Patio,
until the next time at least."

The harness maker grows restless, fumbling
at leather straps, imploring us
to loosen them. In the next bed
Mr. Patio pitches his body
at an angle to ease the pain.
The harness maker works at his straps,
straining to get at the catheter or his balls
to assert ownership of one last province.

My body wants to hibernate;
I remember a plastic Santa Claus

Paul Bennett

whose nose lights up when you pull his bell,
the gift of a bottle of liquor
too precious to drink. I wonder
how it feels when one's back is to the wall,
when the wall dissolves to leaching earth.
Some feet away a flung door slams
upon the familiar universe.

Appalachian Mettle

On Newfoundland Rocks

To the memory of Charles Kirby Potter, born
in Brooklyn, August 6, 1918, drowned off
Newfoundland, February 18, 1942.

I

The sea dispenses time in the North Atlantic—
immense, desolate, gray and white—
where one can never be at home,
where one must always strain to get elsewhere
as fast as possible. And the fastest speed
of the slowest ship governs all ships' speeds
in the naval convoy out of Boston
snaking north northeast, clinging as close as possible
to the rocky coast, running night and day
without lights or radio to frustrate the U-Boat wolves.

As ensign-engineer computing Diesel fuel and RPMs
on the U.S.S. TRUXTUN, Destroyer (of U-Boats) 229,
you found time for facts and memories:
"Some people start off their days by walking
in their gardens; I never feel right
unless I begin mine with a stroll
among turbines, condensers and groves of steampipes.
The other night I dreamed I got your letter,
one of three that somehow reached the ship,
stamped, postmarked, battered. I stood there
turning it over and over, reading the address."

Paul Bennett

II

We but dimly sensed your North Atlantic destiny
on those long sunlit September mornings
in the warmth of Ohio University's Ellis Hall
where you and I first met in 8 o'clock English class.
By common impulse we arrived earlier and earlier
to get our heads straight before Professor Foster
strutted in, took the class roll, climbed
his high chair, flapped his birdy arms,
and began his lecture by aping Chauntecleer.

That freshman English class served us well:
as winter came, we found ourselves at a window
overseeing shadowed campus taking dawn's first light,
exchanging views on Homer, Chaucer, Pound, Eliot,
we toured the classics and the moderns
before a single chair was occupied.

You invited me to your State Street room
to talk about literature. I stayed for lunch.
Our main course was brown bread, broken from the
loaf, and stewed tomatoes, brought to simmer on your
room heater. Dessert was canned peaches, served
after tomatoes in two granite pans. Plain fare, rich talk—
and we decided to room together thereafter.

I learned you were from Long Island, only child
of a father you had never seen, who died
in Army training camp in World War I.
You learned I had two sisters, five brothers,
and visited us in Gnadenhutten, Ohio,

where you exclaimed: "What a family to brother in!"

You umlauted *Gnadenhütten*
—Mother, being German, loved you
for it, and insisted on doing your laundry. At table
you said, "I always wanted to come out west to Ohio
to get an education." "Out west to Ohio?" Father asked.
You tramped the fields with my brothers and me,
hunting arrowheads, digging ginseng and sassafras,
doing all those large-family things that widen eyes.
We showed you the periwinkle that comes in blue,
you knew it in the marble of the sea.

On campus we learned from each other's courses;
I studied history, science, and literature.
You mastered mathematics, languages, and poetry,
then took off your senior year, called to Navy duty;
we joined Phi Beta Kappa together, you *in absentia*.

III

During January, 1942, what North Atlantic seas you
sailed: for three days—you wrote—all we have done
is *hold on*—to bulkheads, bunks, chairs, tables, rails;
we have rolled 58 degrees to either side,
and it felt all of that. Through all the storm
I have not felt well but haven't been seasick either.

On topside the seas rush mountainous:
they come down as though to swamp us,
but the TRUXTUN always lifts into the waves,
gives a good hard roll, and goes over the top.

Paul Bennett

Here in the wardroom the rolling is visible
only in the way the green curtains have
of suddenly standing straight out in midair
then dropping back again. Our stomachs feel it all:
meals have been rations passed out one dish at a time
while we hold ourselves to table or transom

It is some stunt to manage a plate and fork and peas
when sitting on a transom facing athwartships—
to be lifted gently, irresistibly, out of place
by an unusual roll. When this happens
we brace our feet, lean backwards, and skate
across the deck to the table. In three seconds
a reverse roll deposits us back where we started from.
Properly done, this maneuver requires no effort,
but should one step forward at the wrong instant
one goes spinning across the wardroom, fetching up
hard against stanchion or steel bulkhead.

Shaving has much in common with eating on shipboard,
and at sea sensible men let their beards grow;
so far I have shaved every other day
but doing so does not come easy. I brace myself
before a mirror attached to a bulkhead;
as the ship rolls, my reflection swings past in front of me
and I take a quick slash. After a number of rolls
the operation is complete. This sums up
life on the TRUXTUN—my life at least—
just a struggle to *hold on.*

One thing more—something I had never appreciated
before: the immensity of the ocean. I have seen more

desolate and dreary sea since joining the TRUXTUN
than I ever dreamed of. The sea is lifeless
compared to the land. The only visible life
is the seabirds, and I miss animals, buildings, trees.
Winter is rough but not too cold;
we get much wind, rain, spray, but not much snow.

And the worst is that spring—when it comes,
as it surely must—will not be like spring;
we'll see more sun, I'm sure, so that the navigator
won't have to worry about getting his "fixes"
but there won't be any of the awakening
you will see. The North Atlantic will be
as flat and dead as ever.

On February 11 came your Boston postscript:
"At this moment the TRUXTUN is perched
on a marine railway, steady as a rock,
and the riveters' hammers are at work."

IV

Seven days later the TRUXTUN and the POLLUX,
a naval stores vessel in the same convoy,
were pounded to pieces by raging seas
on the rocky south coast of Newfoundland;
the double disaster took place at night
beneath 200 foot granite cliffs of St. Lawrence and
Lawn: snow and sleet obscured navigational aids;
gale-force winds, current-set-to-the-west,
and faulty dead reckoning sent the ships to their doom.

Paul Bennett

Monstrous seas smashed the TRUXTON'S lifeboats
as they were launched. Two crewmen managed to row
a life raft ashore carrying a line
but the line fouled and was ordered cut.
Fishermen of St. Lawrence launched a dory
from the cliff top; their best efforts failed,
the small boat swamped but its crew were saved.
Saved too were 185 members of the two ships' crews,
many deathly sick from frostbite and ingested fuel oil,
pulled from the icy waters and carried up ice-clad cliffs
by brave men and women of St. Lawrence and Lawn.

Most of the crew of the TRUXTUN, which broke up first,
unable to hold on to oil-slick rocks in paralyzing cold,
were washed away before they could be saved.
The total death toll: 203 officers and men,
and you, my chosen brother Charles, among them.

V

Soil is but rock ground fine, finer still from soil
the stuff of flesh, and of flesh, spirit,
so that a mind truly rests in flesh on rock,
and that hard-won, flesh-bound gene pool is person
filtered from out this soil, from out that sea.
You and I, Charles, through three college years
shared the making of two separate persons,
except that we chose to join thoughts and time,
to combine what passed as experience
and to test what we learned by two sets of senses,
two minds. Name it friendship.
As your uncle wrote when you were gone:
"There is this to be said: real friendships are rare."

Appalachian Mettle

But war, our insanity, heaps irony on irony,
mixes "Where am I" with "Who am I."
That wild night your ship ran aground
(hard by the mouth of *Placentia Bay*),
safe in Ohio I beheld two St. Elmo's fires,
the double corposant that would signify
to all who follow the sea "safe passage home."
And your TRUXTUN'S escorting the vessel POLLUX—
once in Athens waltzing past Chubb Library
hand-in-hand double-dating Jeanne and Jenny,
you blithely named us "Castor and Pollux,"
those mythic brothers whose love was destined
to light forever our earth, our sky.

Since the world has no way of knowing
what has been when what has been is gone,
I put pen to paper to say, "Charles, dear friend,
Jeanne and I have stood by your mother
and your Jenny, and we have long since named
our first born son for you." But then I ask:
why were you the one who had to die,
you the last of your bloodline
when there are so many of mine,
the common and lesser kind? And yet,
was it not right that your hard-won person
be reclaimed by the sea from which it came
in such long, fine filtering?

Paul Bennett

On John Yahres' Civil War Diary
(For Andy Yahres Acker)

I

Sturdy iron-roller Union volunteer
begins in a fine firm hand
the brown leather-bound diary
bought of J.R. Weldin, Stationer,
Wood Street, Pittsburgh: "September 2, 1861,
formed the Company in Pine Creek
near the M.E. Church. Called the Mt. Etna Infantry.
Marched to the Orchard, and witnessed
a sword presentation. September 3, 1861,
was today sworn in the service of the U.S.
by Col. Alexander Hayes for three years
or during the war. To receive 13 dollars per month
and 100 dollars bounty, with the benefit
of all pension laws. Left Camp Williams,
Pittsburgh, on September 9. Arrived Washington,
D.C., September 11. Got our breakfast in the
'Soldiers Rest,' and marched to Camp Hays near
the Capitol."

As personal as fingerprints, he sets down
Company C, 63rd Pennsylvania Regiment,
Army of Potomac, officers and men,
weather, roads, railways, rivers, fields,
tents, trees, food, claiming and disbursing
his 13-dollar monthly pay, buying
from farmers cheeses, butter, bread.
"October 4, 1961, Camp Shields, Virginia:
fine morning, rather warm for this time of year.

151

Appalachian Mettle

President Lincoln passed our camp today,
we crowded out to see him. He said
that the time for speaking was past,
that he would speak when the war was over.
October 5, 1861, at 3 p.m. we marched to the
Potomac to wash, we enjoyed ourselves...and felt
much better. November 8, 1861, Camp Johnston,
Virginia: shot at a mark for the first time with
muskets at a distance of 60 yards. Missed the mark."

Practicing war he grows delicate in health,
more delicate with words; and observing enemy
pickets, their red spider camps, rises above hate.
He undergoes countless musters, drills, inspections,
receives a new uniform, new boots, and on January
1 a new Belgian rifle. "For a New Year's gift, I
suppose," he writes, as he records his New Year's
vows: "To live and die a Christian and never to
partake of alcoholic drink."

While Army of the Potomac parries, he travels:
Camp Johnston to Fortress Monroe, to Camp
Hamilton; rejoicing in comrades, letters to and from
home, and at muddy Yorktown that "we agreed to
name 'Camp Misery,'" in *found* second-hand
planking for his tent. More travel, Yorktown to
Williamsburg, and back; Yorktown to Savage's
Station, enduring forced marches, foul weather,
personal illness, until on an overcast day, battle is
joined. The battle rages amid a gathering sense—
winds, clouds, rain—of on-rushing doom.

Paul Bennett

Remanded to the Brigade Hospital with a fever,
he spends his waking hours caring for the wounded.
"June 27, 1862: Heavy cannonading on the right,
with musketry all along the lines. Cook took sick
and I was helping in his place. It is reported this evening
that Jackson has succeeded in turning our right flank.
June 28: Cloudy day. Helped cook breakfast this morning.
Heavy firing of musketry and artillery. The Band nurses
were ordered to the regiment, and I took their place.
Rebels...coming up our rear. I raised the red flag.

"Sunday, June 29: Washed Cooper's sore, cleaned the
room, etc. All who were able, left the hospital,
even our surgeon. Our chaplain, Dr. Marks, stayed
with us. I was determined to stay at all hazards
leaving the future with God. June 30:
Private Williamson of the 105th died last night.
Two scouts came up and took us prisoners...
treated us kindly. I, with the Chaplain and two others,
was left to take care of the sick."

On July 12 under guard by Confederates, who sell him
fresh bread at 16 cents per loaf, he accompanies the
wounded to Richmond, Libby and Son's Warehouse
Hospital. Six days later, weak, feverish, sore, he learns
prisoner exchange is imminent: "I went upstairs to see
Sgt. Whitfield, found him in dying condition, and bid
him farewell. July 19: Cloudy day. Sgt. Wm. P. Whitfield
died at 6 o'clock this morning. The Doctor ordered
all who were able to walk half a mile to start for the
depot. I started at 11:30 a.m., changed cars in
Peterburg. Got aboard the *Vanderbilt* with the
dear old flag above us."

Appalachian Mettle

II

Transported to Bellevue Hospital in New York City,
health and strength are his for taking. "October 9,
1862: Fine day—breakfasted on a chicken and other
good things brought from home by my father. After
which we took a walk down by the harbor."
Laughter, fresh seafood, plentiful fare quicken
blood—his handclasp firm, he entrains for Mt.
Etna, Pennsylvania, to visit family and eat Mother's
cooking. Taking heart from family, friends, a day's
squirrel hunting, he escorts Mother and his sisters to
the city (October 30). "Got our pictures taken at
Glasgow's. I went up to the Provost Marshal's to
report—ordered to Alexandria, Virginia."

He journeys to Harrisburg by train—"Slept in the
cookhouse there, on the soft side of a board"—
and on to Camp Parole at Annapolis, there to be
sent back to his regiment—"old 63rd"—his
Company: "Very glad to see the boys, slept with
Guthrie and Blair in open air."

Again he is tenting, mustering, marching—to
Rappahannock Creek, the camp on Potomac Creek.
"April 10, 1863: President Lincoln and Lady passed
by. He looked cheerful though worn down." On to
Gettysburg —fierce fighting everywhere,
July 1-2-3—July 4: "Cloudy, rained all day, all
quiet. Details made from different regiments to bury
the dead, bring in wounded, gather arms, etc.
Rebels left all in our possession."
The Army marches south—"Slept in straw stack,

fleas plenty"—to Sulphur Springs, Culpepper Court
House, on to Brandy Station. "December 25, 1863:
Another Christmas in the Army—
drunkenness prevailed to a great extent throughout
the Division." Marching, skirmishing, marching, he
proudly asserts: "We made a mile in twelve min-
utes." His brother sends him another brown
leather-bound dairy—bought of John P. Hunt, Book-
seller, Stationer, Masonic Hall, 5th Street, Pittsburgh,
and he sets down a New Year's Resolution for 1864:
"I will faithfully discharge my duty as a soldier and
will faithfully obey all
reasonable orders."

At Chancellorsville, his regiment—old 63rd—took
up the same position held last year, then on May 5,
1864, they marched into the madness of
The Wilderness: amid acrid smoke green woods
churned to mangled brush; shells chopped trees the
size of one's waist to kindling; blood and excrement
plastered earth, wood, leaves, steel. Friends fell, lay
dying, dead, but he himself, unwounded, in forced
marches, dug rifle pits, charged enemy lines:
Spotsylvania, Pole Cat River, North Anna River,
Peninsula, the James River—finally crossed. Dug in,
he is outflanked and captured (June 22, 1864).

III

Guarded by the 1st Virginia, he is led through
Petersburg, all government property seized, hauled
by train to Richmond, marched down main street to
Libby Prison ("found everything remarkably clean"),

and thoroughly searched, then shipped off, deep,
deeper, ever deeper south, to end up (July 11, 1864)
at Andersonville, Georgia. In Andersonville Prison
he reckons with guards, the dreaded dead-line,
thievery, his fellow prisoners—"Six men were hung
inside the prison at 6 p.m. for robbery and murder"
—wretched food, dysentery, vermin, flies, all
nature's calls met in one stream where everyone
must wash, drink, defecate—numbers, the beast in
each let loose.

In homey ways he makes do: "Sewed towels and
stray pieces to form some shelter from the sun, cut
the lining from my coat to close our tent." July
burns out to August. Famished, wracked by illness,
constitutions wrecked, he and thirty thousand
jammed in the fifteen and one-half acre pen, find
every thought dear bought, two-in-one: to live to see
another dawn and home.

Irony marks and masks his anguish: "August 4,
1864: Fine day—no roll call today, prison getting too
crowded to allow room to fall in," as he sets down
the facts: "Monday, August 21, 1864. Cloudy—
rained—a very cold rain today. No rations were
issued to the prisoners. Cause assigned: Tunnels.
Rations to be withheld until they are found out."

And his elation when captured men of Sherman's
Forces bring rumors of Atlanta's fall, prisoner
exchange: "Tuesday, September 13, 1864.
Beautiful day! The prison doors were thrown open
at 6 a.m., and we marched to the station, got on cars

and started to Macon." To Augusta, to Charleston,
S.C.—"sold the buttons from our coats, bought bread."

Held at the Race Course at Charleston, he records, "The
citizens of Charleston treated us with respect—feeding
the hungry, caring for the sick. Seemed like Civil Life
once more—I was put in the 2nd Hundred of the 6th
Thousand, and drew rations."

On October 8, 1864, he is transported by train to
Florence, South Carolina: "Reached our destination
at 7 p.m. Marched out into a field for the night—
very cold and stormy. November 21: Feel very weak
today. Spent the last 20 cents I had (silver), for sweet
potatoes, which made a light dinner—first food we
have tasted for 44 hours. December 6: Consolidated my
socks into one pair, made other improvements in my line
of clothing. December 12: Very cold. Seven of the men
awaiting transportation for exchange are said to have
died from exposure last night."

His 1864 Diary closes with "Resolutions for 1865:
"That I will devote my spare time (while a prisoner)
to reading my Testament.
And that I will endeavor after charity."

IV

Where Diary ends, family legend begins:
in the new year he visits the plantation home
of a nearby South Carolinian family—
is received by them, fed, and cared for
as if he were their war-slain son reborn.

Appalachian Mettle

He regains strength until he is strong enough
to walk. Setting out north he carries
only necessaries: canteen,
one spare shirt and socks,
a brown leather-bound Diary for 1864,
and a piece of white pine stockade—to substantiate
that place where one of three imprisoned died.

Joined by a Pennsylvania friend,
he journeys north through red-clay country
still smouldering, among people still smouldering,
travels much by night, sleeps in hay ricks
and tobacco sheds by day, guided
and aided now and then by freed Blacks—
walking, walking, walking—

Crossing the mountains like a summer sun
to come once more to the heart of his own:
Mother, Father, Sisters, Brothers
(Four years seeded in three small books),
a winter-hardened bud unfolding.

Quotations from *Transcriptions from John M. Yahres' Civil War Diaries, 1861-65* by Andrew Y. Acker. Copyright 1983 by Andrew Y. Acker. Used by permission. All rights reserved.

Paul Bennett

Return to Orchard Hill Spring

The young nurse, solemn in dawn's first light,
ushered the two sons to his bedside. Deftly
she compacted the clutter of steel tubes,
motioned to two chairs, and turned to raise
the window shade. "He sleeps, sometimes he's in,
sometimes he's out. He never speaks."

At the moment he was out, walking the ferny path
that led to Orchard Hill spring. His feet,
for all the intervening years, instinctively
took the slant of hill, his lungs drew deep
the path's minty fragrance, his tongue locked on
the pungent taste of watercress. His breathing
grew difficult and he stopped to rest.

His eyes journeyed ahead, seeking the giant sy-
camore, ready to help it leap from its hollow. His
lips quivered, savoring the water flowing at its
roots; you knew Orchard Hill water
when you tasted it.

The sons took in the wracked breathing, the
shrunken blue-veined skull, the bone-thin arms and
hands, and exchanged glances. The nurse in the
doorway turned. "He has lucid moments, I'm sure,
but he can't speak, as you can see."

The older son, who had been up all night driving
the Interstate, fingered the itching stubble
on his chin, nodded thanks. The younger son,

who had flown into Columbus Airport, leaned close
to his father, patted, caressed a wrist.

The father murmured: "Then as now—"
and was surprised to hear his older son ask,
"Did your old buddy Stake really die
holding up the falling roof of Daisy Hill mine?"

"He did and he didn't." The father smiled.
"If he did, how in God's name would the three of us
be in this automobile, driving back to Owl's Head
to visit Orchard Hill spring? And if he didn't
I wouldn't be here to tell you he held up Daisy Hill
till your uncle Bob and I crawled out from under."

The younger son's mouth trembled, turned down;
he shook his head and looked out the window.
The older son blinked, felt for his handkerchief;
his voice came low: "At least this room is all
Mom would have wanted it to be. Be glad of that."

The father smiled. "Stake died more than once,
you've got to believe that. I saw him standing
like a white oak prop amid dusty shadows
of the Daisy Mine cave-in; and Bob said he rode
shotgun with him and his Patton tank clear across
France into Germany in '44-'45. That same fall I saw
him fending off with his body the fishing vessel
our LST smashed into there in the blue Chesapeake."

He chuckled. "And you both read *The Newark
Advocate*: Stake anchored in midstream the footlog
cable the night Fred hand-walked it across the flooded

Paul Bennett

Raccoon Creek to bring out on his back that old
geezer marooned on his Wolf's Den garage waiting
to drown."

The younger son leaped ahead, walking backwards,
and innocently asked: "Dad, didn't that—all that—
take place *before we had hands?*"

The father whacked his hands together. "Maybe so,
but then as now, blood pulsed in veins like water
flowing from a never-failing spring,
and our feet in motion knew no stop. Running
was our sport, being Stake our game."

The younger son's voice echoed his father's:
"Like as not Orchard Hill spring could have been
named Stake Spring, so says the resident frog,
the three salamanders lying on their damp rock."

The older son smiled. "You two! Dad, what was
your old buddy Stake's real name? You never said."

"His real name?" The father paused. "Well,
I'll tell you if you'll promise not to spread it around.
His real name was *Aconite*, his first name was
Winter. Think of that, being made into a joke at
birth, a yellow, winter-blooming flower whose
leaves gather at the neck like an Elizabethan ruff."

The father peered into his son's face, waiting.
"What chance had Winter Aconite growing up
in Owl's Head, Ohio, during the '20s and '30s?
There where the main employment for grown men

was sitting on the riverbank watching naked boys
learn to dive and swim. The only full-time work
they had was to carve peach seeds into watch fobs,
tell tall tales, and compare their common woes."

The younger son spoke to his brother: "You under-
stand all these things took place in our pokey
Depression town well before we had hands." The
older son sat forward in his chair, hands clasped,
head bowed. He looked up.

The father smiled. "Say, you guys must have heard
this old story: you seem to know it jot and tittle."
The older son looked at his brother, wiped his eyes.
"Never-you-mind," the father said. "In that pokey
town life was a game, with game to be chased, run
down, caught, killed—"

"Cleaned, cooked, and eaten," said the younger son.

The father shook his head. "Well, I never! How do
you guys learn?" Reaching out he hooked his hands
around their boyish necks. "I could knock two
gourds to get an empty echo, but I won't."

Older then younger son ducked free, laughing.
Their escape set the father's hands clapping.
He went on: "Then as now—well before we had
hands—our feet and legs, heart and chest, pumping
arms, teeming brain bonded us in wolf-dog pack to
pursue our game in never-ending marathon. How
else could we evolve this body, this mind, this up-
right two-leggedness—three, counting Stake—our

crazy mix of animal and god,
our talking, killing, caring?"

The younger son looked to his brother, leaned
to the father. "It's *we* and *us* now. His breathing's
harder for less and less." The older son touched his
father's face. "If Mom were here, she'd be saying:
'Stake, dear Stake.'"

"Stake rhymes with snake," announced the father.
"Always has, always will. Your mom knew that,
how *we* became *us*. That woman, that sweet woman!"
He had to smile. "Maybe they rhyme because every
morning of his life a man finds himself tied to a
stake. If he's not being ridden out of town upon a rail
for misbehaving."

The older son cocked an eyebrow at his brother:
"Dad speaks for the youngest squirt among us."
The two brothers laughed and the father joined in;
laughter gave way to coughing, coughing and gasp-
ing. A sudden silence filled the room.

The older son continued to stroke his father's cheek:
the younger son got to his feet, turned to the window.

When the silence became unbearable, the older son
said: "Remember when we three drove back to Owl's
Head and climbed Orchard Hill? Dad wanted one last
visit to that spring. Enroute he insisted on quoting the
first settler's deeds declaring Orchard Hill spring
common property in perpetuity.
How did those deeds read,

they were all worded exactly the same?"

The younger son laid an arm on his brother's
shoulder. "All landowners shall have free and equal
access to said Orchard Hill spring
so long as waters flow."

The older son shook his head. "I remember we found
Orchard Hill itself had been strip-mined, Dad's spring
a sulphurous dribble that had to be led underground
because it stunk and was smelling up School Creek."

"But Dad took it like a man," said the younger son.
"I wish to God we'd got here before his last stroke,
he'd have had some before-we-had-hands story for us."

"Probably some Stake-snake tale," said the older son.
"Do you want to get the nurse, she's the pretty one."

Paul Bennett

The Path: A Fable

I

Wherever it leads
a path follows the sun,
and every traveler, soon or late,
journeys east to west.
Prey to cancer and of that age when
(as Lincoln said)
one must assume responsibility
for one's own face,
Josh Allovus leaves his greening
garden-orchard hillside
and salutes the bright May sun
by walking through Owl's Head
due south, then east.

Following asphalt laid
upon abandoned rail tracks,
accompanied by a quick-winged cardinal,
Allovus passes corn and soybean silos,
the village sewage plant,
Maple Grove Cemetery,
makes a slight, leafy turn
and stands on the wooden bridge
where Tannery Hill Run
enters Raccoon Creek.

There Allovus is stopped cold
by yellow letters on the path:
*Killing is my business
and Business is good.*

He looks around, with reason—
the cardinal has deserted him,
trees and sky are blank. Yellow and blue
yield green, but *this*,
this weds bad to worse,
money-grubbing to death-dealing.

Allovus glances behind to see
if he is being followed:
yes, but only by a black friend,
the widow Sylvia Treat,
making her way slowly
along the path, proudly bearing
a week's supply of groceries
in her familiar fishnet bag.

Allovus moves his feet to cover *killing*
as Sylvia Treat comes abreast:
he asks if he can help her with her load.
She shakes her head. "Thank you, Josh..
I made it from the IGA to here
and I'll make it home for sure."
To the many heads sticking up
in crammed cord bag, she says:
"Whew-ee, you're a load
outside old Sylvia's belly."

As if Allovus were tree or bush
she bends and speaks softly
to progeny in fishnet Bag:
"Skip, you can stay right here
and rest awhile. Ragu,
you stay close with Skip

Paul Bennett

and keep him good company
till old Sylvia comes back this way.
And don't you let him dance on the rail
and fall in that creek, you hear?"

She peers Allovus through, smiles,
then raises the jar of Skippy Peanut Butter
and large size Ragu Spaghetti Sauce,
sets them side by side on wooden bridge rail,
"Old Sylvia will be back this way
come the afternoon,
and don't your forget it. Meantime,
if Josh leaves you alone
you're as safe here as if you stood
in my own kitchen pantry."

Allovus smiles, says, "Sylvia, as always
you amaze and delight me."
Tilting her head to catch water sound,
Sylvia croons: "We go as we go—
                Where, Lord only knows—
                But light as a gosling,
                Loose as a goose, we go."
The fishnet bag of edibles
takes up the rhythm of her body
and she lets it carry her
across the bridge and off the path
toward the house on the hill.

II

Moving Skippy and Ragu
to longer-lasting deeper shade,

Appalachian Mettle

Allovus follows the path
at a slower pace,
pondering man's devious ways,
his own and others' innocence and guilt:
amidst mediocre immediacy
how is one to read an action,
see the farthest reach of it?

And who can claim innocence
when *kill* replaces *piss, shit,* and *fuck*
in graffiti? When Willy Loman peddles Teflon
and *Willie* as in *Willie Horton* begets
in loose-hinged minds the filthiest
of all four-lettered words,
H-A-T-E and F-E-A-R, and these two beget
their natural skin-headed heirs:
Bomb, Burn, Maim, and *Kill*?

Walking the green tunneled path,
wondering, questioning, pondering,
Allovus comes to the cattle farm
where all winter long
he calculated spring's nearness
by counting plastic-covered bales of hay,
seeing eight become seven,
become six, five, three,
dwindle to this last one.
From far off Lake Hudson
there arises the babble of a gaggle
of wild geese. At this distance
they sound like dogs barking,
but in their honking talk they speak
solid sense, the old educating the young.

Paul Bennett

Ah yes, education. Caught without cue cards
might you and I also ask:
"Why do we need school libraries;
I never had one when I went to school?"
Given our bent to skin-headed learning
and laurel-laden athletics, might we not smile
a presidential Teflon smile and say:
"Well, I never tried to be more
than a 'C' student; you see, I had to make
a grade of 'C' to play football."

When notoriety passes as fame
and TV prescience can be practiced
in thirty-second slugs, might you and I not say:
"I will be your education president,
you need read no books; look at me,
read my lips." And you and I too will be
the last to learn that "cheap" education
and "no-tax" preachments defeat
school levies, destroy young minds,
and sap national greatness at its roots.

III

Allovus, who is mongrel Irish,
measures our statesmen-leaders
against Irish Sidhe and ancestors,
those Baltimore slave-holders who,
cushioned in gentle black hands,
left Baltimore County, Maryland,
for the wild Northwest Territory
to be ready to receive
Sylvia Treat's great grandparents

at an underground station,
when crossing Ohio—river and state—
spelled *Canada* and *free*.

History, unlike voters, does not scare
at Willie Horton, does not ride tanks,
pays little heed to words without deeds,
and knows what is done refuses to stay buried
in what is said. Few—a Washington,
a Lincoln, a Franklin D. Roosevelt—
could meld the two. Wrapped howsoever deep
in the tinsel of Grenada, blue waves
of Kennebunkport, history will not blink
will not excuse statesmen who ask only:
"Will it play in Peoria?" History—
and institutions—thank God—
outlive us all.

Overhead on powerful wings
a flight of geese go honking;
natural and perpetual "V"
seven and six in line, honking,
they wheel and head northwest,
pass by their winter home,
head for the sanctuary
of Rutherford's Pond, the far north.

IV

Burdened by a misshaped leg—
whose ache is constant, has been
for weeks—Allovus makes slow headway.
To the right of the path

Paul Bennett

he sees a groundhog burrow,
its several entrances,
snow sealed in early winter,
now open, fresh tracked.
From one, an ageless keen-eyed face
peers, studying him,
curious as he is about what is
and what is to come. Fearful, expectant,
the groundhog holds its ground
long enough to give warning to its kind.

K-I-N-D —Allovus lingers on that word,
makes play of it, gives it play,
makes of it L-O-V-E,
four-lettered antidote to *hate*.
Wiser by wisdom from the ground
(Thoreau would eat a groundhog raw),
Allovus comes to the underpinnings
of the highway bypass bridge,
its concrete sheet a blackboard and easel
for our public spray-painters.

Here Allovus gets his fill
of current four-lettered language-art:
on concrete wall countless males
stand graffiti tall and show
they can cut up Lucy, Denise, Dani,
and diagram several body parts.
They sign themselves Batman, Reggie,
George, William, Bill and Barney.
Allovus deciphers too the fate of "Mary"
(*Hail Mary's* gone awry?),
writ large by Willie and George.

Appalachian Mettle

Allovus wonders: Perhaps these two,
joined by another of their ilk,
accosted young Mary Everett
running this path at dusk last fall,
demanding to know what right she had
to invade their turf, travel their territory,
refuse to bow down in fealty?
Could it have been this trio,
three self-proclaimed macho men,
modeling themselves on big time,
when the lone woman refused to bow, said:
"Like man (like George), by God we took her
in hand and kicked a little ass."

Allovus remembers well the newspaper account:
three young men beating up
and sexually assaulting a lone woman
running a public path at dusk
in rural Ohio—macho macho!
Wherever in this blue world
hate gets a nod in its favor, violence
becomes a business, and business is good!

V

Disheartened but not defeated
Allovus walks on and on
till cancer and fatigue take their toll.
Within sight of the city's corporate sign,
where the wedge of wild geese,
more certain of destiny than he,
whirled honking in the sky,
he turns and heads home,

Paul Bennett

journeying for perhaps the last time
upon a path he has loved well.

He undergoes the purgatorial underpass,
passes by the den where groundhogs
rise on hind legs, whistle, disappear,
comes once more to the green meadow
where Angus-Herefords loll in shade
sharing pasturage, fly-fending tails,
where sails a red-shouldered hawk
that veers, dives, strikes
a mouse-stalking snake. Reflecting
that wild animals and birds of prey kill
only to feed themselves, their young,
Allovus walks on, breathing heavily.

At long last he again stands
on the rude wooden bridge
(Their flag to April's breeze unfurled),
where Tannery Hill Run enters Raccoon Creek.
He smiles, for as if on cue from a master playwright
Sylvia Treat comes strolling, humming,
returning to retrieve her lost children,
her Skippy and Ragu. She stops
and reads aloud the message in yellow:
"Killing is my business
and business is good. Lordy," she says,
"would anybody in right mind think that
unless he was held hostage or slave?"

"Maybe—maybe we are," Allovus says.
"Power enslaves in subtle ways."

Appalachian Mettle

"May—be," Sylvia Treat says, "may—be!"
She raises her eyes to the trees:
"Make us well, set us free."
Tenderly she lifts her children
and lays them in her fishnet bag.
"Now you take care of yourself, Josh,
and let me see you on the path again."

"Ditto, Sylvia," Allovus says, "Ditto to you."

Once more Sylvia Treat leans over the rail
to catch the tune of water meeting water;
she hums, then with assurance begins
a soft song meant for Allovus
and for Skippy and Ragu.

Paul Bennett

Fiftieth Class Reunion

Our class gathers, feeling golden;
our buzzwords are "second family,"
meaning, I suppose, how close
the twenty-six of us became
those dozen years we shared our chance
to learn virtues the world mouths at
but finds so much cotton candy.

Truth is, we stubbornly hung in there
to graduate and kick up our heels
as we met Depression, war, long-clawed time—
the ravishers who ravined our faces,
grayed our hair, bowed our bodies
and stole from our firmament six stars:
Pierce, Stacy, Stan, Etta, Colleen, Gene.

Pierce

Reared in a motherless house
with a manikin mailman for father,
still you carried to our midst
qualities we could only wonder at.
Your signature —so personal— stamped
your every piece of work "excellent,"
and teachers always read your papers first
to have a standard for our class.

You were our valedictorian:
Commencement night as you spoke
heaven and earth hung in perfect balance
and there appeared no limits to your orbit;

only one wise old teacher—Dave Spenser—
demurred: "There is a high school intellect;
Pierce, I fear, has reached his apogee."
How were we to know how right he was?

When war came, you who did so well
in everything you ever tried
could not relax in flying a fighter.
Washed out as pilot, you could not relax
when shooting a star as navigator.
Facing failure for the first time,
mired in Floridian sand, you set your feet
and with one violent sweep of a straight razor
cut yourself free from a wobbling world.

Stacy

Happy realist, trim as an Indian,
child of deep woods and open sky,
you danced among us like a windflower.

Never in this life did I think
I would get to hold you in my arms,
feel your body reply to mine.
Lucky me! Even if it had to be
in our dopey senior class play
before an audience of parents and the guy
you were to welcome to your marriage bed.
Forgive me that I became more fervent
than the role allowed; I did not mean
to make us both forget our lines
or prove you the ad-lib genius you were.

Paul Bennett

Biblically I never got to know you
but by your deeds I knew you well:
when my brother killed your brother
in automobile-motorcycle accident
you became the peace-maker between families;
you stooped to bind our wounds. Later,
seeing you stretched, gaunt, gray, on cancer's rack,
what I would have given to take you
once more in my arms, what wild words
I would have whispered at your ear!

Stan

Because your mind moved as it did,
a trifle slower, oftentimes deeper,
it was not easy for you to be yourself:
simple, loving, sensitive, shy.

I see you still—your eyes tear-filled;
your neck mottled, tense; your mouth pulled two
ways—the snowy December noon your father,
hauling a wagonload of coal with unshod team,
had them slip and fall on the icy roadway
in front of the school. How straddle-legged you
stood as your classmates laughed and jeered your
father who cursed the struggling team,
beat them to their feet.

How far-afield you ran that moonlit night
(Was it autumn of our senior year?) we went coon
hunting and your little mutt roused, fought, and was
bloodied by a huge male coon.
When our flashlight brought back two green eyes

from treed coon, you went berserk:
"Kill him, kill that green-eyed sonofabitch!"

Was it fate or did that shout forecast
your war role in the South Pacific,
the nemesis you became with gun and bottle?
Your story of your Marine buddy
who disappeared during the landing at Guadalcanal:
two days later you stumbled over a helmet
sand-heavy, on the blood frothed beach,
it held your friend's severed head.

Back home you relived that nightmare endlessly;
every time we met the story grew more detailed,
more desperate: "Crabs had got at his nose, his
eyes, his brain was leaching out the bullet hole."
The final tale became the one you told yourself
when in backing down to go to town you ran
your small daughter over. "It's all right,,
I know what to do," you said.

Stan, the price we pay for peace is real
and you paid that price in blood twice over.

Etta

Speedy one, quickest learner, leading reader,
those many years our ready spokesperson—
thinking of you I feel my senses blur.

We're back in the beginning typing class,
you're reporting results of a speed test—
six words off for every error—

Paul Bennett

still you achieve seventy words per minute
while I report my speed at "minus 36."
Then at year's end, our final test,
you turn to me in a stage whisper:
"Do you really want to touch those keys?
At this moment you could report your score
as a gratifying 'even-Steven.'"

Another time I find myself three seats from you
in the darkened, crammed school bus
returning from the Cleveland Great Lakes
Exposition, and you're shouting out my name and
"stop it!" The guys feeling you said you were telling
me something, certainly the teachers, overhearing,
thought so and held my feet to the fire for weeks.

Could it have been, Etta, that you knew
you were destined to die early, and meant to show
how slight were our claims to character,
how fine the line between notoriety and fame?

Colleen

No feminist, you went your quiet Irish way,
tall, graceful, gentle, a smile about to happen.
Many found you diffident; I found you different:
a pussy willow seen in the March distance,
barometer of weather, harbinger of seasons.

Certifiably the luckiest guy in our class
I never found myself Irish blessed
until the wintry day the Shaffner brothers
were painting the school's locker rooms

Appalachian Mettle

and I was told by Coach Bear to dress for gym
in the darkened Home Ec Room. I opened the door
to find you undressing. "Hey," you exclaimed,
"only girls can come in here!" But I was there, and
in the shadows you smiled: suddenly it was spring
with catkins in full bloom.

News of your death, Colleen, came to me at a
distance, changing summer to winter,
but lonelier, colder.

Gene

Had Falstaff got with child the Wife of Bath
we might have seen your equal;
burdened with polio in your youth
you made your twisted foot become your clowning,
your laughter as catching as the common cold.
Your self-declared "Fatso" became "Fats,"
and gave you entry to hearts
where God would have found the going cramped.

What wit and joy could do, you did:
never able to make an athletic team
you made every team as manager,
and kept us sane whatever the score,
however sad our own performance.

When the baseball team, after practice,
invaded the Home Ec Room and devoured
the ham Miss Barnish was baking
for the annual School Board Banquet,
you too pleaded guilty and joined our work party

Paul Bennett

sentenced to police and rake inch by inch
the entire schoolground. I see you yet in obscene
dance, running your hands up and down your tool—
the garden rake lodged between your legs—
surprised by M.C. Snow, the school principal.
"Gene!" he shouted. Then, shaking his head,
smiling: "You belong in Ripley's
Believe It Or Not!"

Your face faking disappointment, you said:
"Sir, I had hoped to make your favorite book
The Twentieth Century Encyclopedia."
Principal Snow, ever the educator said, "Gene,
they've changed the title of that publication
to *The World's Popular Encyclopedia.*"
"Okay," you quipped, "I'll compress to that."

Despite your twisted foot, Gene, in a car
you were by far the best driver among us,
and so it seems right that you departed this earth
from a California parking lot,
your rollicking heart under massive attack
by forces who would haul humor to heaven.

Pierce, Stacy, Stan, Etta, Colleen, Gene—
six stars of first magnitude
brighten our sky this summer night,
confirm our joy on earth, in heaven,
make light the burden of our flesh.
Classmates who delight us from afar,
robed in the grave wisdom you have learned
and we have yet to learn, is darkness what it seems
to be or does memory cause the stars to shine?

Appalachian Mettle

Election Day

Election day—my vote is cast
but I contemplate tomorrow:
given politics and the world's ills,
is a poetic life still possible?

Ezra Pound, whose bent was political,
taste in poetry impeccable,
thought it was. His theory of usury
before he danced the Fascist Follies—
if you have money and need it, use it;
if not, lend it at no interest—
being Christly honest,
would have purged the world
of much managerial graft and stink.
Mussolini, plucking the ego string,
compromised the wishful poet,
and Pound's maundering won for him
a long rest cure in Saint Elizabeth's.

Or take Wallace Stevens creating
the imagined pine, the imagined jay
to make Oxidia livable.
His *Harmonium* in 1924
earned $6.70 in six months' royalties.
He lived for poetry by shuffling papers
in the stacked insurance deck.
Trading on fire and accident's probability,
he guarded his privacy and wrote
what should be but seldom is,
what he knew by strumming the blue guitar:

Paul Bennett

a poet-turned-sailor swims in white water,
roams with tigers in red weather.

II

Risking chaos for night vision
I turn off the TV and lights
and look to blue shadows of the moon:
three pigments of the human eye,
stoked by wave lengths of light,
permit us to distinguish color,
find food and shelter and escape our enemies.
Moon thoughts! From space
astronauts enabled us to see
our precious blue marble
rolling toward the eternal dark.

Close-up we prize variegation:
off Boston I sailed Atlantic gray,
sailed and saw it grow green,
turn wine near Guantanamo,
and once through the Panama Canal
beheld in deep Pacific
those long blue swells that left me
spellbound. Is it possible
to travel among trees on green plains
or better yet, go to sea,
without developing respect for light?

III

Yes it can and has been done.
Years ago in a Veterans Hospital

where doctors with patient deft fingers
labored to replant melted off ears,
noses, eye-lids and lips
on mending red-scar tissue,
I tried not to stare or weep
while the cold tile halls echoed
a poker-playing politician
who some say once went to sea,
as he summoned his toothpaste courage
and told of the sacrifices he had made—
was making to save his nation,
to preserve the integrity
of the highest office in the land.

With a pardon, grant forgiveness.

IV

Gardening, like poetry, sets one free—
thesis proved by William Carlos Williams,
wisest practitioner of them all,
wise enough to come to flowers.
And what if few fresh dollars settle
in this upland gardener's pocket?
I and my gracious woman will not starve
so long as there is soil, rain, and sun.

The two of us cast off berthing lines
and ship out on the late night breeze:
slowly, surely our eyes adjust to stars,
settle upon a garden on an Ohio hill
where words and windfalls freight the air.

Paul Bennett

The Common Path

I

There are some dimensions of death
about which doctors know more than their patients.
Early in September they read my bone scan:
"Prostate cancer metastasized to pelvis, backbone,
and lower ribs. Prognosis: terminal."
Jeanne and I summoned our sons Charlie and Wool
and the four of us readied our house for a siege.
I took counsel of cancer specialists,
began chemo-therapy.

On a sunny October Sunday, as if her body
or brain insisted we stay on the common path
we had traveled for more than half a century,
Jeanne looked up from the New York *Times*' cross-
word puzzle: "I can't fit the letters into the
squares." Nor could she, for she was seeing double
and had lost peripheral vision in her right eye. Our
family physician said: "It appears you've suffered a
slight stroke, but we need you to undergo an MRI
Test just to be sure." Jeanne looked at me and
smiled: "I'll adjust to a slight stroke—and undergo
an MRI if need be." A week later, emerging from
the pounding, claustrophobic MRI tube, she was
told: "You have glioblastoma of the cerebellum,
brain surgery is recommended A.S.A.P."

On November 8, following the three-hour brain
operation, while Jeanne, unconscious, was being
moved to Intensive Care, the woman surgeon met

Charlie and me in the consulting room to inform us the operation was a success: "I got 90 percent of the tumor, and radiation will help with the rest." She paused, studied my face. "But I must tell you, this cancer will prove fatal." The bright consulting room grew huge and dim. Charlie and I stared at one another. Finally Charlie asked: "How long—how long can we expect her to live?" The surgeon met his eyes, nodded, looked away: "I've seen some patients with this kind of tumor survive a year, the average is nearer three months."

With my cancer drugged into what doctors call "remission," I watched Jeanne recover from her operation. Under heavy doses of Decadron she regained coordination and vision, even played her loved Steinway. Charlie and I heard her relate to relatives how good a husband's and son's warm hands felt when, in Intensive Care they enfolded her frigid hands, while she was shivering with cold, stumbling along a deep dark riverbed. The grip of glioblastoma loosened, Jeanne began the prescribed thirty radiation treatments (which got extended to thirty-three). Charlie and Wool and I wondered how devastating it would be when she learned that the cure for which we prayed and for which she locked her body stiff, proudly stiff, in daily radiation therapy, was not a cure at all—would at best let her survive a little while.

Suddenly from tumor or treatments came terrible change: Jeanne began to weaken day by day until she could no longer stand without support;

she had to lock her thinning arms
tight around my neck to enable me to raise her to
her feet. As she weakened further, the doctors
disagreed on what should be the proper dosage of
Decadron. Laboring against brain swelling Jeanne
lost control of her legs, and there came a heart-
wrenching last time she made it up the stairs at
home, me straining, lifting her one step at a time,
and it seemed right to ask if she would prefer to
enter a nursing home where she'd have full-time
professional care. Jeanne smiled as only she could
smile, and reminded me of a neighbor lady who had
said time and again: "Privileged to live in this
blessed countryside next to your gardens, your
orchard, and Jeanne's flowers, you'll see me leave
our house feet first."

I ordered a hospital bed set up in our living room,
signed a Care Star attendant to come once each day,
a nurse to come three times each week, and brought
blankets to make my bed on the sofa beside her.

II

There are some dimensions of death about which
patients know more than their doctors. As Jeanne
lay in her hospital bed in the living room of the
hand-wrought house we had designed and built,
and I sat by her side, she would sometimes protest:
"Oh gee! Oh golly! Oh heck! Oh pshaw!"—wonder-
ful mild oaths that broke my heart. When pain
overwhelmed her she would call out: "Oh Daddy,
Oh Daddy, Oh Daddy, Oh Daddy!

Appalachian Mettle

Oh Charlie, Oh Charlie, Oh Charlie, Oh Charlie!
Oh Wool, Oh Wool, Oh Wool, Oh Wool! Oh John,
Oh John, Oh John, Oh John!"
Her calling for our sons and her dead brother
became her litany of courage, her triumph over
pain. And she made little songs of the words I used
as I tucked her in for the night. Washing the dishes,
doing the laundry, cleaning the house I would hear:
"Cozy and warm, cozy and warm, cozy and warm!"
At night as I settled on the sofa across from her
she would raise a gentle chant: "Peace and quiet,
peace and quiet, peace and quiet." Compelled to
answer her turtle dove song, I would respond:
"Peace and quiet, peace and quiet, it's okay, it's
okay, it's okay," Back would come: "It's okay, it's
okay, it's okay!" until she drifted off to sleep.

Throughout January glioblastoma of the cerebellum
worked its insidious way. On February 1 Jeanne had
a good night, sleeping straight through. At 4 a.m.
she called to me; I moved to her side; she raised her
arms, drew me close, and said: "I am ready...to die."
Later in the morning, fighting the phlegm that
collected in her lungs, she murmured: "I am on the
verge, I am on the verge." Later still as her breath-
ing cleared, she began her litany of courage: "Oh
Daddy, Oh Charlie, Oh Wool, Oh John!" Her pulse
had reached 96, if I read right; in a rising pattern it
soon reached 126 and more.

In that week one bad night followed another. No
longer able to take Decadron or codeine or even
swallow, Jeanne began to suffer chills and fever,

Paul Bennett

drifting in and out of consciousness. In delirium she climbed to her bedroom at 267 Muskingum Drive in Marietta, Ohio, "Head of the stairs to the right," sat again at her study desk, lay again in the antique bed that became our marriage bed. Spring and fall commingled, large west window filled with heady crab apple fragrance, south window with heavy liquorish of ungathered Concords from her Grandfather's grape arbor. Time and again she roller-skated the half mile to Marion Grade School and several times walked back wearing red rubber boots breaking glaze ice in the roadside ditch all the way home.

Once more she rode her bicycle, bike basket loaded with sketching pad and paints, from Forest Street in Cambridge, Massachusetts, to the town of Lynn, only to have the rear bike tire go flat. Short on funds and uncertain of how much the tire repair might cost, she decided to walk her bike the more than twelve miles home. Sun in the sky told her it was two o'clock and she'd have to hurry to make it home before dark. Hurry she did—and wrote her parents all about the lark: that she was safely home and I had mounted a new tire to make the bike as good as new. In her delirium she and Charlie and Wool and I stood at dawn in our hillside raspberry patch as we had done July morning after morning, summer after summer, picking luscious berries and dropping them into cans belted to our waists to allow two-handed picking. Back and forth among the four of us went our antic cries: "Hey Poppa, hey Momma, have you got your bottom covered?"

189

Appalachian Mettle

On February 7 with her pulse rate over 126, delirium gave way to coma, and each breath became a battle against phlegm collecting in her lungs. For more than twenty hours her great heart, toughened by years of hillside gardening, hillside mowing, struggled to keep blood pumping, vital fluids flowing. Near midnight there came a change in her breathing: her mouth closed, breaths came light, almost easy, with longer and longer rests between. Our Black and Tan hound, Rudy, disturbed by the change, sensing something fearsome in the air, circled her bed again and again, and whined. When the sky showed traces of the new day's dawning, Jeanne's breathing faltered, her magnificent heart beat its last. Her travel on the common path was at an end.

About the Author

Paul Bennett has been poet-in-residence at Denison University since 1986, having retired that year as Lorena Woodrow Burke Professor of English. Born in Gnadenhutten, Ohio, and educated at Ohio University and Harvard, he was an officer in the Navy during World War II, and has been by profession a teacher, gardener, orchardist, film writer, novelist and poet. He was a teaching assistant at Harvard and taught in the Samuel Adams School of Social Studies in Boston and at the University of Maine at Orono before joining the Denison University faculty in 1947. In 1973-74 he held a fellowship awarded by the National Endowment for the Arts, and in 1992 received Ohio University's Significant Achievement Award.

Bennett's work has appeared in *The Nation, Georgia Review, The Gamut, New York Times Magazine, Journal of American Folklore, Agni, Loon, Remington Review, Centennial Review, Grecourt Review, Beloit Poetry Journal, College English*, and others. He has published three books of fiction and four collections of poetry, and has scheduled for publication the life story of a remarkable dog: MAX: THE TALE OF A WAGGISH DOG (Mayhaven Publishing, P.O. Box 557, Mahomet, IL 61853).

Paul lives near Granville, Ohio, in the hand-wrought house he and his late wife Jeanne designed and built in 1948.

To order additional copies of

Appalachian Mettle

or receive a copy of the complete
Savage Press catalog,

contact us at:

**Tel: 1-800-732-3867
Voice and Fax: (715) 394-9513
e-mail: savpress@spacestar.com
Web Page**
www.cp.duluth.mn.us/~awest/savpress

Visa or MasterCard accepted.

Savage **PRESS**

Box 115, Superior, WI 54880 (715) 394-9513

We are always looking for good manuscripts—poetry,
fiction, memoirs, family history, true crime and other genres.
Send a synopsis and the first three chapters.

Other Books Available from Savage Press

Hometown Wisconsin by Marshall J. Cook

Treasures from the Beginning of the World by Jeff Lewis

Stop in the Name of the Law by Alex O'Kash

A Hint of Frost — Essays from the Earth by Rusty King

Widow of the Waves by Bev Jamison

Superior Catholics by Cheney & Meronek

Gleanings from the Hillsides by E.M. Johnson

Keeper of the Town by Don Cameron

Thicker Than Water by Hazel Sangster

Moments Beautiful Moments Bright by Brett Bartholomaus

The Courtship of Sarah McClean by S & S Castleberry

Some Things You Never Forget by Clem Miller

The Year of the Buffalo,
a novel of love and minor league baseball
by Marshall J. Cook

Pathways by Mary B. Wadzinski

Beyond the Mine — The Pete Benzoni Story by Pete Benzoni